Wadsworth's Guide

to

Careers in Criminal Justice
Third Edition

Caridad Sanchez-Leguelinel
John Jay College of Criminal Justice

THOMSON

™

WADSWORTH

Australia • Canada • Mexico • Singapore • Spain • United Kingdom • United States

Printed in United States

   3 4 5 6 7 10 09 08 07

Printer: Thomson West
ISBN-13: 978-0-495-13038-3
ISBN-10: 0-495-13038-9

Thomson Wadsworth
10 Davis Drive
Belmont, CA 94002-3098
USA

For more information about our products,
contact us at:
Thomson Learning Academic Resource Center
1-800-423-0563

For permission to use material from this text or product,
submit a request online at
http://www.thomsonrights.com.
Any additional questions about permissions can be
submitted by email to **thomsonrights@thomson.com.**

Caridad Sanchez-Leguelinel, Ph.D. is an Assistant Professor and the Associate Director of the Department of Counseling at John Jay College of Criminal Justice – City University of New York (CUNY). Professor Sanchez-Leguelinel is the author of numerous articles focusing on college student development, and facilitator of professional lectures that assist students in developing the skills, awareness, and experience necessary to prepare for careers in the Criminal Justice field.

TABLE OF CONTENTS

Chapter 1: INTRODUCTION

Welcome to Wadsworth's *Guide to Careers in Criminal Justice, Third Edition*. This text will provide you with a brief introduction to the dynamic field of criminal justice, including the most common professional positions, recent employment trends, and some useful job-finding strategies. It is intended to help criminal justice students and other individuals who are considering a career in the field get an overview of potential jobs they might want to pursue. This guide will give you the "big picture" of careers in criminal justice. From this perspective you can then narrow your focus and create a plan for attaining your short- and long-term career goals.

This text does not, however, attempt to provide an exhaustive exploration of all topics and issues relevant to careers in criminal justice. For more information and guidance, we suggest you consult *Seeking Employment in Criminal Justice and Related Fields, Fourth Edition* by Harr and Hess (Wadsworth). Another useful tool is Wadsworth's *Careers in Criminal Justice* interactive CD-ROM, release 3.0. We also encourage you to take advantage of the many web sites listed in the text which provide direct information regarding job descriptions, vacancies announcements, and hiring procedures. Lastly, take advantage of the career resources offered by your college, university, community center, local library, and/or area government offices.

Finally, a text such as this one can only do so much. It's up to you to get out there and explore. Talk to as many people as you can who work in the criminal justice field. If possible, arrange to observe them at work. Write letter, attend lectures and conferences, and participate in criminal justice-related events. In other words, *get involved*. That's what criminal justice is all about.

THE CRIMINAL JUSTICE SYSTEM

This section provides a brief overview of the three main areas of the criminal justice system—law enforcement, the courts, and corrections. Each of these areas receives full-chapter treatment later in this text (see Chapters 2, 3, and 4).

As you read this section and later chapters, keep in mind that there is significant interaction and cooperation among these three groups. For example, if you work in law enforcement, odds are you will deal with correctional and court personnel quite often. Some jobs effectively straddle the line between two areas. Bailiffs, for example, are officers (usually deputy sheriffs) who are assigned to facilitate the court process. While some are sworn, armed law enforcement officers, others are not. Duties of the bailiff include maintaining order in the court and assisting courtroom participants. So, if you are interested in both law enforcement and the court system, perhaps you should consider a career as a bailiff. The point is to be open to the many possibilities that await you.

Law Enforcement
Like the other two areas of criminal justice, law enforcement represents a wide diversity of career opportunities. While patrol officers, detectives, and sheriffs are still the foundation of law enforcement, dozens of police specialties have emerged at all levels of government and private organizations. These include Federal Air Marshals, Postal Inspectors, and Pretrial Service Officers, just to name a few.

Please note this text treats private security personnel—including private detectives and guards—as part of the law enforcement environment. While these personnel may not be sworn officers, they are an important and rapidly growing feature of the law enforcement landscape. One important thing to remember is that working in private security can lead to future opportunities in government-based law enforcement. The opposite is also true. An example is the significant number of police officers who have traded in their badges to become private detectives.

Government-based law enforcement is divided into four different levels or *jurisdictions*—federal, state, county, and local.

The Federal Government maintains a high profile in many areas of law enforcement. *Federal Bureau of Investigation (FBI) agents* are the Government's principle investigators, responsible for investigations of violations of more than 200 categories of Federal law, and conducting sensitive national security investigations.

U.S. Drug Enforcement Administration (DEA) agents enforce laws and regulations relating to illegal drugs. Not only is the DEA the lead agency for domestic enforcement of Federal drug laws, it also has sole responsibility for coordinating and pursuing U.S. drug investigations abroad.

U.S. Marshals and Deputy Marshals protect the Federal courts and ensure the effective operation of the judicial system. They provide protection for the Federal judiciary, transport Federal prisoners, protect Federal witnesses, and manage assets seized from criminal enterprises.

Bureau of Alcohol, Tobacco, Firearms, and Explosives agents regulate and investigate violations of Federal law relating to firearms, explosives, arson, and alcohol and tobacco diversion.

The U.S. Department of State *Bureau of Diplomatic Security special agents* are engaged in the battle against terrorism.

The *Department of Homeland Security* employs numerous law enforcement officers under several different agencies, including *Customs and Border Protection, Immigration and Customs Enforcement*, and the *U.S. Secret Service*.

U.S. Border Patrol agents protect more than 8,000 miles of international land and water boundaries.

Immigration inspectors interview and examine people seeking entrance to the United States and its territories. They inspect passports to determine whether people are legally eligible to enter the United States.

Customs inspectors enforce laws governing imports and exports by inspecting cargo, baggage, and articles worn or carried by people, vessels, vehicles, trains, and aircraft entering or leaving the United States.

Federal Air Marshals provide air security by fighting attacks targeting U.S. airports, passengers, and crews. They disguise themselves as ordinary passengers and board flights of U.S. air carriers to locations worldwide.

U.S. Secret Service special agents protect the President, Vice President, and their immediate families; Presidential candidates; former Presidents; and foreign dignitaries visiting the United States. Secret Service agents also investigate counterfeiting, forgery of Government checks or bonds, and fraudulent use of credit cards.

Other Federal agencies employ police and special agents with sworn arrest powers and the authority to carry firearms. The agencies include the Postal Service, the Bureau of Indian Affairs Office of Law Enforcement, the Forest Service, and the National Park Service, just to name a few.

Most federal agencies have state counterparts, such as the State Bureau of Investigation and Apprehension. Perhaps the most familiar state law enforcement job is that of State Trooper (State Police and State Highway Patrol). Some state police enforce all state laws while others enforce only traffic laws on major roadways. Other state agencies include the Department of Natural Resources, Fire Marshal Division, Driver and Vehicle Services Division, and Department of Human Rights.

County agencies with law enforcement responsibilities include the County Sheriff, the County Police, and the County Coroner/Medical Examiner. At the local level, career opportunities can be found in township, municipalities, and special district police departments. Other local positions include Constable and Marshal.

The Courts

When most of us think about people who work in the courts, we immediately think of lawyers and judges. While these are the two highest-profile positions in the judicial system, a large cast of supporting characters is needed to keep the system running. These include paralegals, court administrators, legal assistants, court clerks, bailiffs, and court reporters.

Like law enforcement professionals, lawyers can work in the private or public sector. In the public sector, attorney positions exist at the federal, state, county, city, and town level. Thanks to movies and television, the most familiar government lawyer is the district attorney, who represents "the people" in criminal cases. On the opposing side you may find the public defender, another government employee who provides legal counsel to defendants who cannot afford a private defense attorney.

Private attorneys work in an increasingly diverse array of specialty areas. These include corporate, insurance, personal injury, bankruptcy, divorce, and real estate law, just to name a few, Recent societal and business trends have created strong demand for lawyers who specialize in immigration, technology, patent, communications, and labor/ employment law. Public interest law remains a popular sub-field despite decreased funding for many legal service programs.

One major difference between lawyers (many of whom eventually become judges) and other criminal justice professional is the level of schooling required. While many law enforcement and correctional positions require only an associate's degree (if even that), all lawyers must have a bachelor's degree and a law school degree. For most people, this means at least seven years of post-secondary study, including the intensely competitive challenge of getting into (not to mention completing) law school and passing the bar examination.

Unlike lawyers, all judges are government employees. There is no such thing as a private judge. Some judgeships, such as Supreme Court Justice, are appointed posts, while others are elected positions. Again, judges may work at the federal, state, county, city, or town level.

The court system also relies on the services of psychologists, social workers, case managers, and other counselors. Because these individuals are usually brought in after sentencing, this text treats them as part of the correctional system.

Corrections

When most of us think of corrections, we think of prison guards. While the majority of people who work in this sub-field are correctional officers, jailers, or other custody-related personnel (such as wardens), additional opportunities exist as well. As stated above, counselors of many types are brought in to help rehabilitate and manage convicted criminals. Because juvenile crime (especially violent juvenile crime) continues to rise, counselors who specialize in working with youths are in high demand. And with the growing popularity of so-called "drug courts" for addressing drug-related crime, substance abuse specialist will find an increasing number of opportunities in the correctional system.

As is the case in law enforcement and the courts, correctional workers can work at the federal, state, county, or local level. This is not to say, however, that all aspects of the correctional system are wholly government operated. Private companies are now being brought in to construct, staff, and manage many different types of correctional facilities. Of course, the government is still responsible for what goes on in these privately operated facilities, but working conditions for corrections officers and other personnel may vary between private and public facilities.

Parole and probation officers represent two other exciting job opportunities in corrections. While community-based corrections is a volatile issue in many states (some of which have eliminated these kind of programs), the number of parolees and probationers nationwide continues to rise, as does the demand for law enforcement and the courts to ensure that parolees and probationers re-enter society without compromising community safety.

Now let's take a closer and more detailed look at the three main areas of the criminal justice system previously discussed: Law Enforcement, the Courts, and Corrections.

Chapter 2: CAREERS IN LAW ENFORCEMENT

INDUSTRY CONDITIONS AND EMPLOYMENT STATISTICS

Introduction

According to the U.S. Bureau of Statistics' *Occupational Outlook Handbook* 2006-2007 Edition, employment of police, detectives, and special agents in the U.S. (both public and private) is expected to increase faster than the average for all occupations through 2014. However, within the law enforcement field itself, job availability can vary greatly depending on a number of factors, the most obvious of which is a high incidence of crime. The *Occupational Outlook Handbook* reported that the largest number of employment opportunities will arise in urban communities with relatively low salaries and high crime rates. The following data, provided by the Bureau of Justice Statistics (2006), summarizes the opportunities and trends in federal, state, and local law enforcement agencies.

General Law Enforcement Statistics

In 2000, there were nearly 800,000 full-time sworn law enforcement officers in the United States.

Type of agency	Number of agencies	Number of full-time sworn officers
Total		796,518
All state and local	17,784	708,022
Local police	12,666	440,920
Sheriff	3,070	164,711
Primary state	49	56,348
Special jurisdiction	1,376	43,413
Texas constable	623	2,630
Federal*		88,496

Note: Special jurisdiction category includes both state- and local-level agencies. Consolidated police-sheriffs are included under local police category. Agency counts exclude those operating on a part-time basis.
*Non-military federal officers authorized to carry firearms and make arrests.

Federal Law Enforcement Statistics

- As of June 2002, federal agencies employed more than 93,000 full-time personnel authorized to make arrests and carry firearms.

- Of all federal officers, 14.8% were women and 32.4% were members of a racial or ethnic minority.

- The largest employers of federal officers, accounting for 60% of the total, were the:

  - Immigration and Naturalization Service (19,101)
  - Federal Bureau of Prisons (14,305)
  - U.S. Customs Service (11,634)
  - Federal Bureau of Investigation (11,248)

- About half of all federal officers were employed in

  - Texas (13,374)
  - California (12,315)
  - District of Columbia (8,114)
  - New York (7,202)
  - Florida (5,963)

- Nationwide, there were 32 federal officers per 100,000 U.S. residents, including 1,421 per 100,000 residents in the District of Columbia. There were more than 50 per 100,000 residents in Arizona, New Mexico, Texas, Alaska, Hawaii, and Vermont. There were fewer than 10 per 100,000 in Wisconsin, New Hampshire, and Iowa.

State and Local Law Enforcement Statistics

Personnel

- As of June 2000, state and local law enforcement agencies had 1,019,496 full-time personnel, 11% more than the 921,978 employed in 1996. From 1996 to 2000 the number of full-time sworn personnel increased from 663,535 to 708,022.

- As of June 2000, local police departments had 565,915 full-time employees including about 441,000 sworn personnel. Sheriffs' offices had 293,823 full-time employees, including about 165,000 sworn personnel.

- From 1987 to 2000, minority representation among local police officers increased from 14.5% to 22.7%. In sheriffs' offices, minorities accounted for 17.1% of sworn personnel in 2000, compared to 13.4% in 1987.

- From 1996 to 2000, total employment by local police departments was up an average of 2.1% per year. Sheriffs' offices increased their number of employees by 3.5% per year.

Education and Training Requirements

- In 2000, 15% of local police departments and 11% of sheriffs' offices had some type of college education requirement for new officers.

- In 2000, new local police recruits were required to complete an average of about 1,600 hours of academy and field training in departments serving 100,000 or more residents, compared to about 800 hours in those serving a population of less than 2,500. New deputy recruits in sheriffs' offices serving 100,000 or more residents were required to complete an average of 1,400 hours of training compared to about 780 hours in those serving a population of less than 10,000.

Law Enforcement Training Academies

- As of year end 2002, a total of 626 state and local law enforcement academies operation in the United States, offered basic law enforcement training to individuals recruited or seeking to become law enforcement officers.

- An estimated 53,302 trainees successfully completed or graduated from their training program.

- An estimated 17% of recruits who completed training in 2002 were female and 27% were members of a racial or ethnic minority.

Changing Education Requirements

As many criminal justice agencies upgrade their educational requirements for employment, higher education becomes an extremely vital commodity. As a general rule, the bachelor's degree has become the minimal entry-level requirement for most criminal justice positions. Even in the field of "uniformed law enforcement," which has not traditionally required a college degree for entry level employment, is moving in the direction that seeks to establish a certain number of required courses (and one could expect eventually, a college degree) to become eligible for employment. Across our nation, we have also witnessed an increase in the number of colleges offering degrees in the criminal justice and related fields, which supports the notion that a college degree is taking on increased value. In fact, pursuing a graduate or law degree after a bachelor's degree, is also encouraged as a vehicle to make you more competitive for career employment and for advancement within many criminal justice agencies.

NEW TRENDS IN LAW ENFORCEMENT

Keeping up to date of the structural changes within our federal government, as well as targeted recruiting efforts, is key to understanding the emerging directions within law enforcement. Below are two trends worth notice:

U.S. Department of Homeland Security

It became evident after the tragic events of September 11 that our country must be more adequately prepared to secure our Nation from acts of terrorism. In efforts to insure the safety of our country, the federal government created the U.S. Department of Homeland Security (DHS).

The primary reason for the establishment of the Department of Homeland Security was to provide a unifying core for the vast national network of organizations and institutions involved in efforts to secure our Nation. In order to better do this and to provide guidance to the 180,000 DHS men and women who work every day on this important task, the Department developed its own high-level strategic plan.

Mission Statement

"We will lead the unified national effort to secure America. We will prevent and deter terrorist attacks and protect against and respond to threats and hazards to the nation. We will ensure safe and secure borders, welcome lawful immigrants and visitors, and promote the free-flow of commerce."

Strategic Goals

Awareness: Identify and understand threats, assess vulnerabilities, determine potential impacts and disseminate timely information to our homeland security partners and the American public.

Prevention: Detect, deter, and mitigate threats to our homeland.

Protection: Safeguard our people and their freedoms, critical infrastructure, property and the economy of our Nation from acts of terrorism, natural disasters, or other emergencies.

Response: Lead, manage and coordinate the national response to acts of terrorism, natural disasters, or other emergencies.

Recovery: Lead national, state, local and private sector efforts to restore services and rebuild communities after acts of terrorism, natural disasters, or other emergencies.

Service: Serve the public effectively by facilitating lawful trade, travel and immigration.

Organizational Excellence: Value our most important resource, our people. Create a culture that promotes a common identity, innovation, mutual respect, accountability and teamwork to achieve efficiencies, effectiveness, and operational synergies.

Department Subcomponents and Agencies

The following list contains the major components that currently make up the Department of Homeland Security:

Directorates and Components:

The *Directorate for Preparedness* works with state, local, and private sector partners to identify threats, determine vulnerabilities, and target resources where risk is greatest, thereby safeguarding our borders, seaports, bridges and highways, and critical information systems.

The *Directorate for Science and Technology* is the primary research and development arm of the Department. It provides federal, state and local officials with the technology and capabilities to protect the homeland.

The *Directorate for Management* is responsible for Department budgets and appropriations, expenditure of funds, accounting and finance, procurement; human resources, information technology systems, facilities and equipment, and the identification and tracking of performance measurements.

The *Office of Intelligence and Analysis* is responsible for using information and intelligence from multiple sources to identify and assess current and future threats to the United States.

The *Office of Operations Coordination* is responsible for monitoring the security of the United States on a daily basis and coordinating activities within the Department and with Governors, Homeland Security Advisors, law enforcement partners, and critical infrastructure operators in all 50 States and more than 50 major urban areas nationwide.

The *Office of Policy* is the primary policy formulation and coordination component for the Department of Homeland Security. It provides a centralized, coordinated focus to the development of Department-wide, long-range planning to protect the United States.

The ***Domestic Nuclear Detection Office*** works to enhance the nuclear detection efforts of federal, state, territorial, tribal, and local governments, and the private sector and to ensure a coordinated response to such threats.

Federal Emergency Management Agency (FEMA) prepares the Nation for hazards, manages federal response and recovery efforts following any national incident, and administers the National Food Insurance Program.

Transportation Security Administration (TSA) protects the nation's transportation systems to ensure freedom of movement for people and commerce.

Customs and Borders Protection is responsible for protecting our nation's borders in order to prevent terrorists and terrorist weapons from entering the United States, while facilitating the flow of legitimate trade and travel.

Immigration and Customs Enforcement (ICE), the largest investigative arm of the Department of Homeland Security, is responsible for identifying and shutting down vulnerabilities in the nation's border, economic, transportation and infrastructure security.
Federal Law Enforcement Training Center provides career-long training to law enforcement professionals to help them fulfill their responsibilities safely and proficiently.

Citizenship and Immigration Services is responsible for the administration of immigration and naturalization adjudication functions and establishing immigration services policies and priorities.

The ***U.S. Coast Guard*** protects the public, the environment, and U.S. economic interests – in the nation's ports and waterways, along the coast, on international waters, or in any maritime region as required to support national security.

The ***U.S. Secret Service*** protects the President and other high-level officials and investigates counterfeiting and other financial crimes, including financial institution fraud, identity theft, computer fraud; and computer-based attacks on our nation's financial, banking, and telecommunications infrastructure.

Career Opportunity Areas

The Department of Homeland Security has unique career opportunities that will challenge your mind and reward your skills and talents. As a Homeland Security employee, you will help secure our borders, airports, seaports, and waterways; research and develop the latest security technologies; respond to natural disasters or terrorists assaults; and analyze intelligence reports.

Office of the Secretary – employees work in multiple offices contributing to the overall Homeland Security mission.

Directorate for Preparedness – employees work with state, local, and private sector partners to identify threats, determine vulnerabilities, and target resources where risk is greatest, thereby safeguarding our borders, seaports, bridges and highways, and critical information systems.

Directorate for Management – employees work in one of a variety of critical areas, from human resources and administration to budgeting, procurement and IT, making certain the right resources and systems are in place to achieve Homeland Security's mission.

Directorate for Science and Technology (S&T) – employees plan, fund, and manage top-flight research and development programs in almost all technical fields to ensure that our Nation's federal, state, and local responders have the scientific resources and technological capabilities that they need to protect our homeland.

Office of Intelligence and Analysis – employees use information and intelligence gathered from multiple sources to identify and assess current and future threats to the United States.

Office of Inspector General – employees work side-by-side with special agents, attorneys, engineers, and IT experts to prevent and detect fraud, waste, and abuse in Homeland Security programs and operations.

U.S. Citizenship and Immigration Services (USCIS) – employees are responsible for adjudicating and processing the host of applications and forms necessary to ensure the immigration of people and their families to the United States, from initial stages through their transition, to permanent residence, and finally to citizenship.

U.S. Coast Guard – civilian employees work together with military personnel to save lives, enforce the law, operate ports and waterways, and protect the environment.
To find out how you can join us in this vital mission, visit the U.S. Coast Guard website: http://www.gocoastguard.com

U.S. Customs and Border Protection (CBP) employees prevent terrorists and terrorist weapons from entering the United States while facilitating the flow of legitimate trade and travel.

Federal Emergency Management Agency (FEMA) – employees prevent losses from disasters wherever possible, and assist when they do happen. You will be part of an intensely-focused team dedicated to helping our country prepare for, prevent, respond to, and recover from disasters.

U.S. Immigration and Customs Enforcement (ICE) employees enforce immigration and customs laws, safeguard U.S. commercial aviation, and protect Federal facilities.
U.S. Secret Service – employees have the dual missions of protecting our Nation's leaders, and criminal investigation involving law enforcement, security, information technology, communications, administration, intelligence, forensics, and other specialized fields.

Women and Diversity in Law Enforcement

In order to gauge the status and growth of women in law enforcement, the National Center for Women and Policing (2002), conducted a comprehensive study on women sworn officers and civilian personnel within the largest law enforcement agencies in the United States. In addition, a second annual survey of small and rural law enforcement agencies was conducted by the Justice and Safety Center at Eastern Kentucky University, in cooperation with the National Center for Women and Policing.

The results of both studies indicate that the number of women in law enforcement has increased at an alarmingly slow rate over the past 30 years. The findings conclude that women continue to remain severely under-represented in large, small and rural law enforcement agencies.

Below are the key findings of this report which provides a clear, yet discouraging picture of where women are in law enforcement today.

- Women currently comprise 12.7% of all sworn law enforcement positions among large municipal, county, and state law enforcement agencies in the United States with 100 or more sworn officers. Women of color hold 4.8% of these positions.

- In small and rural police agencies, women hold only 8.1% of all sworn positions. Women of color are virtually absent, with a representation of 1.2%. For this survey, small and rural police agencies are defined as those country and municipal agencies located in a county with a population of less than 50,000 and with fewer than 100 sworn personnel.

- Over the last ten years, the representation of women in large police agencies has slowly increased from 9% in 1990 to 12.7% in 2001 – a gain of less than 4%. This under-representation of women is striking, given that women account for 46.5% of the adult labor force.

- There is now mounting evidence that the slow pace of increase in the representation of women in large police agencies has stalled or even possibly reversed. The percentage of women in large police agencies was 14.3% in 1999, 13.0% in 2000, and 12.7% in 2001. This discouraging trend is primarily concentrated among municipal and state agencies, and raises the question of whether women will ever reach equal representation or gender balance within the police profession.

- Within large police agencies, sworn women currently hold only 7.3% of top command positions, 9.6% of supervisory positions, and 13.5% of line operation positions. Sworn women of color hold 1.6% of top command positions, 3.1% of supervisory positions, and 5.3% of line operations positions.

- In small and rural agencies, sworn women hold only 3.4% of all top command positions, 4.6% of all supervisory positions, and 9.7% of all line operations positions. Women of color represent less than one percent of both top command positions (0.3%) and supervisory positions (0.4%) and only 1.5% of all line operation positions.

- More than half (55.9%) of the large police agencies surveyed reported no women in top command positions, and the vast majority (87.9%) reported no women of color in their highest ranks. For small and rural agencies, 97.4% have no women in top command positions and only 1 of the 235 agencies has a woman of color in their highest ranks. This is a clear indication that women continue to be largely excluded from the essential policy-making positions in policing.

- Among those police organizations with at least 100 sworn personnel, state agencies trail municipal and county agencies by a wide margin in hiring and promoting women. Specifically, state agencies report 5.9% sworn women law enforcement officers, which is significantly lower than the percentage reported by municipal agencies (14.2%) and county agencies (13.9%).

- One possible explanation for the stall or even decline in women's representation within sworn law enforcement is the decrease in the number of consent decrees mandating the hiring and/or promotion of women and/or minorities. Among surveyed agencies, eight consent decrees were implemented since 1995, and only six were implemented in the entire decade. Without the consent decrees imposed to remedy discriminatory hiring and employment practices by law enforcement agencies, even the marginal gains women have made in policing would not have been possible.

Clearly, the grave disparity between the numbers of men and women involved in policing, adversely impacts the culture, operations, and efficacy of law enforcement agencies throughout the country. Given the many difficult challenges facing modern police agencies, the imperative to hire more women has never been more urgent.

THE JOBS

This section provides basic information about twenty common law enforcement positions. Each jobs entry including a brief general description, basic employment requirements, salary/benefits information and contact information. To learn more about these and related position, we encourage you to contact the agencies and organization listed.

BUREAU OF ALCOHOL, TOBACCO, FIREARMS AND EXPLOSIVES SPECIAL AGENT

Description
The ATF enforces federal laws and regulations relating to alcohol, tobacco, firearms, explosives and arson to suppress and prevent crime through enforcement, regulation, and community outreach. Special Agents are responsible for investigations relating to illegal activities involving arson, firearms, alcohol products, and tobacco. Agents function to insure consumer and industry compliance with laws and regulations of these products. These activities can include surveillance, collection of evidence, raids and searches, and arrests. Agents often submit their reports to the U.S. Attorney for use in the cases.

Requirements
U.S. Citizen.
Between the ages of twenty-one and thirty-seven.
Pass panel interview and background investigation.
Medical examination and drug screening.
Valid driver's license.
Must have a college degree or have one of the following requirements:
GS-5: Three years investigative or enforcement experience related to criminal violations.

GS-7: One year experience equivalent to the GS-5 level and leadership/membership of an organization dealing with investigations.

Training
Ten weeks of training at the Federal Law Enforcement Training Center, Glynco, Georgia, and another seventeen weeks of specialized training. First year of employment serves as a probationary period.

Salary and Benefits
GS-5 to GS-9: Base salary range $31,075 to $39,448.
Salary range excludes locality pay and the 25% law enforcement availability pay. Federal benefits typically include sick and annual leave, health and life insurance, and retirement plans.

Contact Information
Bureau of Alcohol, Tobacco, Firearms, and Explosives
Personnel Division
650 Massachusetts Avenue NW, Room 4100
Washington, DC 20226
202-648-9100 Recruitment and Hiring Center
www.atf.treas.gov

U.S. Office of Personnel Management
1900 E. Street NW
Washington, D.C. 20415
www.opm.gov
www.usajobs.opm.gov

Source: Bureau of Alcohol, Tobacco, Firearms, and Explosives
U.S. Department of Labor, Bureau of Labor Statistics, *Occupational Outlook Handbook* 2006-2007 Edition

CANINE ENFORCEMENT OFFICER

Description
Customs Canine Enforcement Officers train and use dogs to enforce customs laws and regulations that pertain to the smuggling of controlled substances, i.e., marijuana, narcotics and dangerous drugs, as well as weapons, explosives, merchandise, agricultural products and contraband in

motor vehicles, mail, aircraft, unaccompanied baggage, and cargo ships. One of the unique aspects of the Customs Canine Program team is working with explosives detector dogs. Duties may include checking packages in and processing passengers at airports. Canine Enforcement Officers are authorized to carry firearms and make arrests. The law enforcement efforts are often coordinated with Customs Inspectors and other federal, state and local enforcement agencies.

Requirements
U.S. Citizen.
Eyesight tests will assess distant visual acuity and near vision (correction permitted).
Applicants must be able to hear the spoken voice at 20 feet.
Appointments to GS-5 level requires Bachelor's degree.
Experience in law enforcement (for positions above GS-5).
Training
Canine Enforcement Officers attend a Basic Narcotics Detention course which includes instruction in canine behavior and handling, detection of drugs, and search techniques.

Salary and Benefits
For GS-5 level, salary begins in the upper $20,000's.
For GS-7 level, upper $20,000's to upper $30,000's.
Benefits include health and life insurance, and retirement plans.

Contact Information
www.customs.ustreas.gov
888-USA-DOS1

Source: United States Customs Service, U.S. Department of the Treasury

DRUG ENFORCEMENT ADMINISTRATION SPECIAL AGENT

Description
Responsibilities include complex investigations involving violations of the Controlled Substances Act. This may include surveillance and undercover operations to expose drug operations, such as drug trafficking, and seizing illegal substances and evidence pertaining to the violations. Special Agents commonly work with other federal, state, and local agencies and are

authorized to carry weapons, make arrests, execute warrants and serve subpoenas. This position requires the possession of firearms and can be hazardous. After sixteen weeks of training, agents are placed on three to four years of probation.

Requirements
U.S. Citizen.
Twenty-one years of age but not older than thirty-six.
BA Degree for GS-7 position.
Valid driver's license.
Good physical condition (including vision and hearing).
Superior academic achievement, graduate education, and experience, enhances the application and permits appointment at higher GS-levels.

Training
Training consists of eight weeks at the Federal Bureau of Investigation's Academy in Quantico, Virginia. Instruction includes ethics, self-defense, use of firearms, law, court procedures, criminology, investigative techniques, drug identification, etc. Applicants are also required to pass physical condition testing.

Salary and Benefits
Beginning salary at the GS-5 level is mid to upper $20,000's (not including locality variance pay) plus 25% overtime compensation. Contact the local recruiter for detailed description of benefits.

Contact Information
Drug Enforcement Administration
2401 Jefferson Davis Highway
Alexandria, VA, 22301
800-DEA-4288
www.usdoj.gov/dea
Source: Drug Enforcement Administration

FEDERAL AIR MARHSAL

Description
Federal Air Marshals (FAM) respond to criminal incidents aboard U.S. air carriers, as well as other in-flight emergencies. Marshals are authorized to

carry firearms and make arrests, while preserving the safety of aircraft, crew, and passengers. Marshals conduct investigations, inspections to enhance security and work collaboratively with other federal, state, and local law enforcement officers and airport/airline officials. FAMs perform regular and extended travel, both domestic and foreign. Work hours and shifts are irregular.

Requirements
U.S. Citizen; under the age of thirty-seven.
Must pass physical/drug test/top secret clearance.
Perform regular/extended travel and spend time in foreign countries where terrorist activity is considered likely.
FV-G: BA/BS degree or three years of general experience in administrative, professional, technical or investigative areas, or
FV-H: Three years of graduate education in criminal justice, public administration, police science, law or aviation management, or specialized experience equivalent to FV-H level.

Training
Candidates hired in FAM positions must take/pass criminal investigation course held at the Federal Law Enforcement Training Center. The training includes pass/fail components based on classroom instruction, physical fitness, and firearms training.

Salary and Benefits
Starting salary $35,100 to $80,800. In addition, positions are covered by the 25% law enforcement availability pay. Salary adjusted to include locality.
FAA Core Compensation: Effective April 23, 2000, the FAA adopted a new pay system for Federal Air Marshal positions. These positions are now in the Technical job category under Core Compensation. Positions formerly at the FG-5/7/9 grade levels are now in Level 1, pay band G; positions formerly at FG-11/12 grade levels are now in level 2, pay band H; and positions formerly at the FG-13 grade level are now in level 3, pay band I.

Contact Information
Federal Aviation Administration
Department of Transportation
800 Independence Ave SW
Washington, D.C. 20591
866-835-5322
http://jobs.faa.gov

Source: Federal Aviation Administration

FEDERAL BUREAU OF INVESTIGATION AGENT

Description
The FBI is the primary investigative arm of the federal government.
Responsibilities include enforcing federal statutes and conducting national
security investigations. Activities include investigations into organized
crime, white-collar crime, public corruption, financial crime, fraud against
the government, bribery, copyright infringements, civil rights violations,
bank robbery, extortion, kidnapping, air piracy, terrorism, foreign
counterintelligence, interstate criminal activity, fugitive and drug-
trafficking matters, and other federal statute violations. One of the FBI's
top investigative priorities is to protect the United States from terrorist
attacks and from cyber based and high technology crimes. Headquarters
are located in Washington DC, offices are also located throughout the U.S.
and worldwide. FBI agents are authorized to carry weapons, make arrests,
execute search warrants, and serve subpoenas.

Requirements
U.S. citizen or a citizen of the Northern Mariana Islands.
Twenty-three years of age minimum, no older than 36.
Willing to relocate.
Uncorrected vision no worse than 20/200 and corrected 20/20 in one eye,
20/40 in other. Must pass a color vision test.
Pass medical examination for physical fitness and meet proportioned
weight/height ratio.
Must possess a valid driver's license.
Four-year degree from a higher education accredited college or university.

Applicant can apply to any of the four areas below:
Law: must have earned a juris doctorate degree.
Accounting: B.S. degree in accounting and has passed the CPA or must take the FBI's accounting exam.
Language: must be proficient in at least one foreign language.
Diversified: three years full-time work experience or an advanced degree plus two years work experience.

Prior history is considered during the employment process and applicants can be disqualified for prior records such as a conviction of a major misdemeanor or felony, illegal drug use, failing a drug screening or polygraph.

Training
Special Agents are required to attend sixteen weeks of training at the FBI Academy in Quantico, Virginia. Training includes learning defense tactics, how to use firearms, physical fitness, and practical application exercises. After training is complete, first assignment for an Agent usually lasts four years.

Salary and Benefits
Agents will enter the GS pay scale at GS-10 level (field work, non-supervisory) which ranges from $43,441 to low $70,000s with availability pay up to 25% of their grade scale.

Benefits include health and life insurance, full retirement plans, and vacation and sick pay.

Contact Information
1. Fill out written application that can be downloaded from www.fbi.gov/employment/agent4.htm
2. Written test
3. Interviews
4. Background investigation includes checking educational achievements, personal and business contacts, credit history, and prior arrest history

Federal Bureau of Investigation
935 Pennsylvania Avenue, NW, Room 7972
Washington, DC 20535
202-324-3000
www.fbi.gov

Sources: Federal Bureau of Investigation
U.S. Department of Labor, Bureau of Labor Statistics, *Occupational Outlook Handbook* 2006-2007 Edition

FEDERAL POLICE OFFICER – U.S. GENERAL SERVICES ADMINISTRATION

Description
The Federal Protective Service represents the law enforcement arm of the Public Buildings Service, U.S. General Service Administration. Federal officers enforce federal laws through patrol, apprehension of criminals, and investigation of crimes. Responsibilities include responding to incidents and emergencies, traffic control, collecting evidence, conducting investigations of a GSA controlled property, and assisting state and local police as needed.

Requirements
Valid driver's license.
United States Citizen.
Pass background screening and physical exam.
Must have a bachelor's degree, or experience in law enforcement equivalent to the next lower grade level.

Salary and Benefits
Average starting salary in upper $20,000's – mid $30,000s.

Contact Information
U.S. Office of Personnel Management
1900 E. Street NW
Washington, DC 20415
www.opm.gov

www.usajobs.opm.gov
Source: U.S. Office of Personnel Management

FISH AND WILDLIFE SPECIAL AGENT

Description
The U.S. Fish and Wildlife Service, an agency of the Department of the Interior, has responsibility for the protection, maintenance, and control of fish and wildlife resources. Fish and Wildlife Special Agents are responsible for ensuring that wildlife shipments entering or leaving the United States comply with federal wildlife trade laws and international treaties, and to intercept illegal shipments of federally protected wildlife. Duties include examining wild animals, packages, crates and other containers transported by air, sea, and land; carried by individuals or through the mails, as well as the examination of documentation that accompanies shipment. Fish and Wildlife Special Agents participate in investigations and provide expertise to other agencies in wildlife law, testify in court, and inspect wildlife imports and exports. The duties involve considerable travel and frequent periods away from regular stations.

Requirements
U.S. citizen must be between twenty-one and thirty-seven years of age. Must pass a test that measures memory and powers of observation. Comprehensive physical examination.

Training
Those appointed to the U.S. Fish and Wildlife Service attend a Wildlife Inspector training program at the Federal Law Enforcement Center in Glynco, Georgia. Following formal training, candidates are assigned to a designated law enforcement office for on-the-job training.

Salary and Benefits
Entry level is at the GS-5 level, beginning mid to upper $20,000's (BA/BS degree or three years experience); for GS-7, beginning mid to upper $30,000's, one full year of graduate education, or superior academic achievement during undergraduate studies. For GS-9, a master's degree or two years of graduate experience.

Contact Information
U. S. Fish and Wildlife Service
1849 C Street, NW
Washington, DC 20240

USFWS Customer Service Center
800-344-WILD

Source: United States Fish and Wildlife Service.

INDUSTRY OPERATIONS INVESTIGATOR

Description
The Industry Operations Investigators are the backbone of the Bureau of
Alcohol, Tobacco, Firearms, and Explosives (ATF). Work is primarily
investigative and routinely involves inspections pertaining to the industries
and persons regulated by ATF. Investigators identify evidence of
falsification of records and inventories, and document discrepancies
through the analysis of records and reports. Conduct interviews, inspect
buildings, and perform routine background investigations to determine
suitability of persons wishing to enter business in the regulated industries.
Assist in criminal investigators on alcohol and tobacco diversions.

Requirements
U.S. Citizen.
Between the ages of twenty-one and thirty-seven.
Physically capable to perform duties.
Background investigation for top secret clearance.
Pass panel interview.
Valid driver's license.
Medical exam.
Drug screening.
Must have a college degree or have one of the following requirements:
GS-5: Three years investigative or enforcement experience related to
criminal violations.
GS-7: One year experience equivalent to the GS-5 level and
leadership/membership of an organization dealing with investigations.

Training
Ten weeks of training at the Federal Law Enforcement Training Center,
Glynco, Georgia. First year of employment serves as a probationary period.

Salary and Benefits
GS-5 to GS-9: Base salary range $25,195 to $38,175.
Salary range excludes locality pay and the 25% law enforcement
availability pay. Federal benefits typically include sick and annual leave,
health and life insurance, and retirement plans.

Contact Information
Bureau of Alcohol, Tobacco, Firearms, and Explosives
Personnel Division
650 Massachusetts Avenue NW, Room 4100
Washington, DC 20226
202-648-9100 Recruitment and Hiring Center
www.atf.treas.gov

U.S. Office of Personnel Management
1900 E. Street NW
Washington, D.C. 20415
www.opm.gov
www.usajobs.opm.gov

Source: Bureau of Alcohol, Tobacco, Firearms, and Explosives
U.S. Department of Labor, Bureau of Labor Statistics, *Occupational
Outlook Handbook* 2006-2007 Edition

INTELLIGENCE SPECIALIST

Description
Intelligence Operations Specialists and Intelligence Research Specialists are
employed in a wide range of agencies. At the U.S. Department of Defense,
Intelligence Specialists of the Naval Criminal Investigation Service perform
intelligence analysis relative to criminal investigations, counterintelligence,
and terrorism activities in support of Navy and Marine operations
worldwide. At the Federal Bureau of Investigations, Intelligence Research
Specialists are responsible for the interpretation of national security

information in support of the criminal intelligence, foreign counterintelligence, counterterrorism, and organized crime missions of the F.B.I. United States Border Patrol Intelligence Research Specialists are responsible for producing and analyzing immigration intelligence, and the Bureau of Alcohol, Tobacco, Firearms, and Explosives, employs Intelligence Research Specialists to conduct complex analytical studies. Intelligence Research Specialists are also employed by the Financial Crimes Enforcement Network of the U.S. Department of the Treasury where they disseminate intelligence information gathered from a number of data bases to assist in building investigations, preparing prosecutions, combating money laundering and other financial crimes. Intelligence Research Specialists are also employed by the U.S. Customs Service and the Drug Enforcement Agency.

Intelligence Operation Specialists of the United States Immigration and Nationalization Service are responsible for gathering and interpreting information relating to the smuggling of aliens, immigration fraud, and counterfeiting of immigration and other identity documents. Operation Specialists are also employed by the Bureau of Intelligence and Research of the U.S. Department of State for the coordination of sensitive civilian and military intelligence operation for the Department and other federal agencies. Intelligence Operations Specialists serve as the liaison on operation intelligence related to counterterrorism with the intelligence community, the National Security Council, and relevant State Department bureaus.

Requirements
Applicants must be U.S. Citizens.
Requirements for Intelligence Specialist appointments to GS-5 level include completing of a four-year course of study leading to a bachelor's degree, OR three years general experience, one year of which was equivalent to GS-4; for GS-7, one full year of graduate education, or superior academic achievement during undergraduate studies, OR one year of specialized experience equivalent to GS-5.

Training
Contingent upon the agency hired for, in-service training will include subjects related to specific duties of the position.

Salary and Benefits
Salary appointment at GS-5 level ranges from $22,000 to $28,000; GS-7 from $27,000 to $35,000; GS-13 from $57,000 to $74.000.

Contact Information
U.S. Immigration and Naturalization Service
Department of Justice
425 I Street, NW
Washington, DC 20536

Civilian Personnel Management Division
U.S. Coast Guard
2100 Second Street, SW
Washington, DC 20536

Drug Enforcement Administration
Washington, DC 20537

Federal Bureau of Investigation
Washington, DC 20535

Source: U.S. Office of Personnel Management (OPM)

INTERNAL REVENUE SERVICES SPECIAL AGENT

Description
Internal Revenue Services Special Agents investigate violations of federal tax laws and conduct other investigations relating to the Department of the Treasury. Work involves surveillance, participation in raids, interviewing witnesses, interrogation of suspects, searching for physical evidence, serving search warrants, and inspecting records and documents. Agents organize and present evidence to U.S. Attorneys and testify in court. They must be proficient in the use of firearms, skilled in unarmed defense, and be able to exercise judgment, resourcefulness and initiative.

Requirements
U.S. Citizen, not older than 37 years of age.

Successful passing of Treasury Enforcement examination medical and drug testing required. Valid driver's license. Must pass background investigation and an interview.
GS-5 level: BA/BS degree which includes courses in accounting, finance, economics, tax/business law or money and banking or combination of education and business experience that involves knowledge and application of accounting, auditing, and general business practices.
GS-7 level: one year graduate education with courses in finance, economics, etc., OR meet superior academic standard (high GPA) or combination education and experience as related to investigations of criminal violations involving the use of skills in the area of accounting, auditing, business, and tax law.

Training
Selectees spend approximately 21 weeks of training at the Federal Law Enforcement Center in Glynco, Georgia. Failure to successfully complete the course of basic training is grounds for dismissal. Extensive class and in-service training while on the job is provided to enhance performance and career advancement.

Salary and Benefits
Salary ranges from low $40's to mid $50's for GS 5-7 levels. GS-9 low $50's to low $60's with additional potential cost of living allowances. Regular and recurring overtime/travel.

Contact Information
Internal Revenue Service
Department of Treasury
1111 Constitution Avenue, NW
Washington, DC 20224
202-622-5000
www.irs.treas.gov
www.jobs.irs.gov

Source: Internal Revenue Service

MUNICIPAL POLICE OFFICER

Description
Police Officers are responsible for upholding laws, promoting public safety, providing services, and maintaining order within given jurisdictions. Typical duties include gathering information and evidence when responding to incidents and emergencies, reporting suspicious activities, logging daily work, communicating with community members to promote peace and safety, apprehending suspects and intervening crimes, ensuring that federal, state, and local laws and ordinances are upheld, and enforcing traffic laws. Patrol can be facilitated by foot, bicycle, horse, motorcycle, boat, or car. Police work can be dangerous and requires an officer to be armed. Shifts can occur twenty-four hours a day and may include weekend and holiday work. Overtime compensation is given, usually at 25% of salary.

Requirements
U.S. Citizen.
Twenty years of age (varies by department) may also have an age limit (thirty-five to forty years of age).
Physically fit, including good vision, health, and strength.
High school diploma or equivalent (many federal and local police departments may have higher education requisites).
No prior felony convictions.

Training
Training for police academy recruits varies and usually takes between three to seven months; upon graduation, a probation period is served under a field officer. Most departments require continuous education to keep abreast of the changing needs in law enforcement.

Salary and Benefits
Variances depend on locality and overtime compensation.
Median annual earnings of $45,210 in May 2004. The lowest 10% earn $26,910, and the highest, $68,880.
Standard benefits include sick and vacation accrual, pension and retirement packages, and medical and life insurance.

Contact Information
Contact your local police department for employment opportunities.

Source: U.S. Department of Labor, Bureau of Labor Statistics, *Occupational Outlook Handbook* 2006-2007 Edition.

POSTAL INSPECTOR

Description
The U.S. Postal Service has an investigative agency that focuses on all postal operations and illegal activities involving the mails. Investigations focus on crimes such as mail fraud, mail theft, possession of stolen mail, assaults upon Postal personnel, burglary of Postal facilities, robbery of letter carriers, bombs and explosives sent through the mails, trafficking in narcotics and other controlled substances through the mails, counterfeiting of postmarks and postage stamps, theft of postal money orders and postage stamps, and use of the mails to distribute child pornography and money laundering. Inspectors work closely with other federal agents in efforts to halt such traffic, and in this work they have statutory power of arrest.
In audit investigations, inspectors determine whether postal revenues are being properly protected, funds are spent economically and the Postal Service is operating in the best interest of the public. Inspectors conduct comprehensive and objective audits that result in recommendation for improvements, cost reduction and maximum managerial effectiveness in mail handling, data systems, customer services, financial operations, and outside contracts. Finally, the Inspector must be ready to respond to catastrophic situations such as floods, fire, and air or train wrecks to ensure the safety and recovery of postal valuables, property and personnel.

Requirements
U.S. Citizen, between the ages of 21 and 37.
Ability to prepare clear and concise reports.
Enhanced qualifications include: language skills, postal experience, academic achievement, and specialized non-postal experience.
Bachelor's degree. Speak, read and write well.
Willing to relocate.

Training
Postal Inspectors attend a sixteen-week basic training program at the Postal Inspector Training Academy in Potomac, Maryland.

Salary and Benefits
Salary for this position does not fall under the General Schedule pay system although it is similar to the GS-11 Special Agency position of other agencies. Salary range from upper $30,000's to mid $70,000's.

Contact Information
U.S. Postal Inspection Service
475 L'Enfant Plaza, SW
Washington, D.C. 20260
www.usps.gov/websites/depart/inspect/

Source: U.S. Postal Inspection Service

PRIVATE DETECTIVE/INVESTIGATOR

Description
Private investigators and detectives are usually employed by public and private organizations and government agencies to protect their businesses and employees, but are also hired by people searching for missing persons. Investigations may include gathering evidence for trials, tracing debtors, and conducting background investigations. Investigators often specialize in legal (assisting with civil litigation), corporate (internal and external) investigations, including white-collar crime, and store detection (loss control and asset protection). They also provide assistance in civil liberty and personal injury cases, insurance claims and fraud, child custody cases and fraud. In all cases, private investigators assist attorneys, businesses, and the public with legal, financial, and personal problems.

Requirements
Education and licensing varies between states. Minimum education is a high school diploma, although positions often require college experience, majoring in criminal justice, or law enforcement/ investigations experience. Screening can include a background investigation, fingerprinting, and a test for investigation aptitude.

Training
Training and licensing varies by state and employer.
Some states have no state-wide licensing regulations.

Salary and Benefits
The median annual earnings of salaried private detectives and investigators were $32,110 in 2004, approximately $60,000 at high end. Corporate employers usually provide benefit packages.

Contact Information
U.S. Office of Personnel Management
1900 E. Street NW
Washington, DC 20415
202-606-1800
www.opm.gov
www.usajobs.opm.gov

Source: U.S. Department of Labor, Bureau of Labor Statistics, *Occupational Outlook Handbook* 2006-2007 Edition

PRIVATE SECURITY GUARD

Description
Private Security Guards are hired by private businesses, transportation facilities, and public operating organizations to monitor the flow of people entering and leaving, surveying for breach of security, illegal behavior, overseeing crowd control, and protecting property. The position may be one involving constant interaction with people or conducted alone (typically at night). Guards use handheld radios to communicate with other guards on duty, video and metal detectors to detect suspicious activity, and computers to track occurrences. Patrol functions are conducted on foot, at a central entrance way or by vehicle to survey the perimeters of property. In 2000,1.1 million jobs in private security existed.

Requirements
Eighteen years old.
Background check.
Good hearing and vision, physically fit.
Drug screening.
Federal jobs require a written exam and firearm competency.

Training
Federal jobs require firearms training; armed guards in generally receive more training.
Most states require that guards be licensed.

Salary and Benefits
Average salary $20,320 in May 2004.
Lowest average $16,640.
Highest $33,270.

Contact Information
Contact private businesses directly or check the U.S. Office of Personnel Management job listing at www.usajobs.opm.gov.

American Society for Industrial Security
1625 Prince Street
Alexandria, VA 22314-2818
703-519-6200
www.asisonline.org

Source: U.S. Department of Labor, Bureau of Labor Statistics, *Occupational Outlook Handbook* 2006-2007 Edition

SHERIFF

Description
County Sheriffs are responsible for enforcing federal, state, and local laws in the specified county of jurisdiction. Those duties involve the enforcement of traffic laws, apprehending suspects, conducting investigations, responding to emergencies, facilitating county jails, transporting pre-sentenced and sentenced individuals, patrol, custody and court control, and serving warrants and court orders. Sheriffs and deputy sheriffs are usually elected to their posts and perform duties similar to those of a local or county police chief. Sheriff's deputies who provide security in city and county courts, are sometimes called Bailiffs.

Requirements
High school diploma or equivalent.

Most county agencies require applicants be twenty years of age.
U.S. Citizen.
Valid driver's license.
Excellent physical condition (meet vision, hearing, and height/weight ratio).

Training
Sheriffs' departments typically conduct training over a period of weeks or
months, and train cadets in emergency response, report writing, laws and
applications, use of firearms, investigations and physical conditioning.

Salary and Benefits
Salary ranges depending on locality and prior experience. Upper $20,000's
to mid $60,000's. Medium earnings are $44,750 in federal government.
Benefits typically include sick and vacation leave, health and life insurance,
and retirement plans.

Contact Information
Contact your local county sheriff's office for employment opportunities.

National Sheriffs' Association
1450 Duke Street
Alexandria, VA 22314
www.sheriffs.org

Source: U.S. Department of Labor, Bureau of Labor Statistics,
Occupational Outlook Handbook 2006-2007 Edition

HIGHWAY PATROL OFFICER/STATE TROOPER

Description
Highway Patrol Officers/State Troopers maintain public safety and enforce
laws on highways, interstates, freeways and other terrain within their state
jurisdiction. Officers enforce vehicle and traffic laws by monitoring
automobile speeds, auto theft, transportation of illegal contraband,
responding to emergency situations, conducting investigations, assisting
motorists, searching and seizing persons, automobiles and evidence,
conducting investigations, and appearing in court. State officers are also
responsible for enforcing all criminal laws and often respond to accidents

and emergencies that occur beyond highways, freeways, and interstates. State Law Enforcement agencies operate in every state except Hawaii. Seventy percent of Troopers function as uniformed officers and the remainder are divided between investigative, court, or administrative duties.

Requirements
Must possess a high school diploma or equivalent (varies by state).
Valid driver's license.
No prior criminal history.
U.S. Citizen.
Nineteen to thirty-one years of age.
Good physical condition (visual, hearing, height/weight ratio, dental).
Written examination.
Pass physical and psychological testing, and polygraph test.

Training
Training is conducted at state academies where trainees will be educated on criminal and vehicle laws, penal codes, enforcement procedures, emergency vehicle operations, investigation, firearm training, emergency response, and traffic control.

Salary and Benefits
Salary ranges from $34,410 to $56,360. Starting salary depending on locality (does not include overtime compensation).
Benefits typically include sick pay, annual leave, health and dental plans, and retirement/pension benefits.

Contact Information
Contact your state's police/highway patrol department for employment opportunities. You can find contact information for all 50 states at:
www.sover.net/~tmartin/State/htm

Sources: U.S. Department of Labor, Bureau of Labor Statistics, *Occupational Outlook Handbook* 2006-2007 Edition

UNITED STATES BORDER PATROL AGENT

Description
Responsibilities include the detection, prevention, and apprehension of illegal aliens trying to enter the United States of America. Activities include night and day surveillance using various technologies, tracking leads and any suspicious activities that may lead to the apprehension of illegal aliens and/or smugglers of aliens or contraband. Agents are required to learn Spanish and carry a weapon. Agents work closely with other federal, state, and local agencies.

Requirements
U.S. Citizen.
Valid driver's license.
Entry level testing: verbal skills, knowledge of Spanish language or an assessment of language aptitude, and prior experience assessment.
Physically conditioned.
Pass drug testing.
Must have good vision (including color vision).
To qualify for the GS-5 level: minimum of one year of federal service work experience at the level of GS-4 or substituted college experience.
To qualify for the GS-7 level: minimum of one year of law enforcement work experience equivalent to the GS-5 level requirements or one year of graduate education (law enforcement related).
Those applicants holding a bachelor's degree and high academic achievement may be applicable to apply at the GS-7 level.
Initial location can be anywhere.

Training
Agents attend an eighteen-week Border Patrol academy at the Federal Law Enforcement Training Center in Glynco, Georgia. Must pass qualifying exams in the Spanish language and immigration laws.

Salary and Benefits
Salary at the GS-5 level begins at upper $20,000's.
Salary at the GS-7 level begins at mid $30,000's.
Salaries listed above do not include compensation for overtime.
Salary may increase to $50,000 by the fifth or sixth year of employment.
Benefits include health and life insurance, savings and retirement plans.

Contact Information
U.S. Border Patrol
Bureau of Customs and Border Protection
425 I Street NW
Washington, DC 20536
800-238-1945
www.ins.usdoj.gov

U.S. Office of Personnel Management
1900 E. Street NW
Washington, DC 20415
www.opm.gov
www.usajobs.opm.gov

Source: U.S. Border Patrol

UNITED STATES CAPITOL POLICE OFFICER

Description
U.S. Capitol Police Officers are responsible for the safety of Congressional members and their families, protecting the safety of life and property, criminal investigations, and enforcing traffic laws in congressional buildings and parks. Future opportunities exist in the areas of protective services, investigations, emergency response, hazardous devices, K-9 communications, electronic countermeasures and specialized patrol. United States Capitol Police officers are often called upon to work with the Secret Service.

Requirements
Between the ages of twenty-one and thirty-seven.
Possess a high school diploma or equivalent.
U.S. Citizen.
Physically fit. Pass vision and hearing tests.
Valid driver's license.
No record of felony conviction.

Training
Twenty-one weeks of field officer training. Training takes place in Washington and in Glynco Georgia at the Federal Law Enforcement

Training Center. Training includes physical defense, customs search and seizure, criminal and customs law, police procedures, laws and arrest, and behavioral sciences.

Salary and Benefits
Starting salary $48,354-$56,119, after training salary.
Benefits include sick and annual leave, life and health insurance, and retirement plans.

Contact Information
U.S. Capitol Police
Recruiting and Investigations Section
119 D Street, NE
Washington, DC 20510
866-561-USCP

U.S. Office of Personnel Management
1900 E. Street NW
Washington, DC 20415
www.opm.gov

Source: U.S. Office of Personnel Management

UNITED STATES CUSTOMS INVESTIGATOR

Description
Responsible for investigating issues related to drug or weapon smuggling, money laundering, and customs fraud. Investigations include surveillance, interviews, and collection of evidence and immediate searches of persons, merchandise, and vehicles. Must be willing to work long hours, be armed, and be willing to relocate.

Requirements
U.S. Citizen.
Pass drug screening and medical testing, including hearing and vision exams.
Background investigation.
To attain the GS-5 level, you must have three years work experience involving law enforcement or law violations or a minimum of one year's

experience at the GS-4 level. A bachelor's degree may be substituted for work experience.
To attain the GS-7 level, you must have either one-year experience in investigations or intelligence, or one year of experience equal to the GS-5 level (undergraduate scholastic achievement and/or graduate education may satisfy this requirement).

Training
Sixteen weeks of required training at the Federal Law Enforcement Training Center in Glynco, Georgia.

Salary and Benefits
Salary at the GS-5 level $25,822 to $41,585.
Salaries listed above do not include compensation for overtime.
Benefits include health and life insurance, savings and retirement plans.

Contact Information
Check with your local Office of the Special Agent-in-Charge for vacancies.

U.S. Customs Service
Office of Human Resources
P.O. Box 14156
Washington, DC 20044
www.customs.gov
www.usajobs.opm.gov/dhscareers/

U.S. Customs and Border Protection
1300 Pennsylvania Avenue
Washington, D.C., 20229
www.cbp.gov

Source: U.S. Department of Homeland Security

UNITED STATES CUSTOMS SERVICE INSPECTOR

Description
U.S. Customs Inspectors are responsible for searching cargo, ships, aircraft, automobiles, and people for illegal importation and exportation of weapons,

contraband, and stolen property. Customs Inspectors conduct personal interviews and conduct searches on cargo
Ships, planes, and motor vehicles leaving the United States. Other duties include assessing taxes, duties, and penalties to property being imported and exported. Borders include Mexico, Alaska, Hawaii, and the Islands of the Caribbean. Inspectors are stationed in over 300 ports of entry in the United States.

Requirements
U.S. Citizen.
Possess a valid driver's license.
Pass drug and medical testing, including hearing and eyesight examinations.
To attain the GS-5 level, you must have a college degree from an accredited four-year institution or three years work experience or a combination of college education and work experience equaling three years.
Willing to work in a variety of geographic locations.

Training
Prospective inspectors are required to participate in eleven weeks of training at the Federal Law Enforcement Training Center in Glynco, Georgia, which includes physical conditioning and the use of firearms.

Salary and Benefits
Salary at the GS-5 level begins in the upper $20,000's.
Salary at the GS-7 level begins in the mid $30,000's.
Salaries listed above do not include compensation for overtime.
Benefits include health and life insurance, savings and retirement plans.

Contact Information
U.S. Customs Service
Office of Human Resources
P.O. Box 14156
Washington, DC 20044
www.customs.gov
www.usajobs.opm.gov/dhscareers/

U.S. Customs and Border Protection
1300 Pennsylvania Avenue
Washington, D.C., 20229
www.cbp.gov

UNITED STATES IMMIGRATION DEPORTATION OFFICER

Description

Deportation Officers are responsible for the control and removal of persons who have been ordered deported or required to leave the United States. Officers closely monitor deportation proceedings from inception to conclusion and serve in a liaison function to foreign consulates and embassies to insure the efficient issuance of passports and other travel documents required for deportation. Deportation Officers investigate and apprehend aliens who have absconded and provide protective security when needed.

Requirements

U.S. Citizen.

Minimum 21 years of age and no older than 37 (unless previous service credits under special law enforcement provision).

Must pass background investigation, drug screening/physical exam.

GS-5 level: BA/BS degree or three years experience

GS-7 level: one year graduate education or specialized experience and/or superior academic achievement during undergraduate studies. Combination of education and experience are reviewed to determine eligibility.

Foreign language proficiency a plus.

Training

Attending 13-week basic training course at Federal Law Enforcement Training Center in Glynco, Georgia; training in foreign language proficiency and in-service course in deportation processing, immigration law/deportation processing, firearms, and arrest procedures.

Salary and Benefits

Starting at GS-5 level: start mid $20,000's; GS-7 upper $20,000's to low $40,000's.

Benefits covered under Federal Employees Retirement System

Contact Information
U.S. Immigration and Naturalization Service
Department of Justice
425 I Street, NW
Washington, D.C. 20536
202-514-2690
www.immigration.gov

Source: U.S. Department of Homeland Security

UNITED STATES IMMIGRATION INSPECTOR

Description
Responsible for monitoring admission of people into the United States of America, and verifying appropriate documents and claims regarding immigration and naturalization laws. At many points of entry, Immigration Inspectors search aircraft, cargo, and motor vehicles entering the country. Inspectors perform as uniformed, armed law enforcement officers that respond to crimes and make arrests.

Requirements
U.S. Citizen.
Possess a valid driver's license.
Pass drug screening and medical testing.
Bachelor's degree or current federal employee or experience.
Must pass written test.

Training
Immigration Officer's Basic thirteen-week Training Course at the Federal Law Enforcement Training Center in Glynco, Georgia, including instruction in immigration and nationality law, and proficiency in the Spanish language.

Salary and Benefits
Salary at the GS-5 level begins at upper $20,000's.
Salary at the GS-7 level begins at mid $30,000's
Salaries listed above do not include compensation for overtime.
Federal benefits typically include health and life insurance, savings and retirement plans.

Contact Information
Immigration and Naturalization Service
Department of Justice
Division of Recruiting
PO BOX 9317
Arlington, VA 22219
www.ins.usdoj.gov

U.S. Office of Personnel Management
1900 E. Street NW
Washington, DC 20415
www.opm.gov

Source: U.S. Department of Homeland Security

UNITED STATES IMPORT SPECIALIST

Description
U.S. Import Specialists regulate what products are allowed for importation, enforce laws relating to fair trade, intellectual property rights, and public health and safety; and help define and institute trade agreements. Import Specialists determine admissibility, classification, and duty to be paid for goods that enter the United States.

Requirements
U.S. Citizen.
Pass drug screening and medical testing.
Background investigation.
To attain the GS-5 level, you must have three years work experience or a minimum of one year's experience at the GS-4 level. A bachelor's degree may be substituted for work experience.

Training
Required five weeks of technical training at the Federal Law Enforcement Training Center in Glynco, Georgia, which covers the examination of laws and regulations pertaining to the appraisal of merchandise, custom duties, and other topic areas.

Salary and Benefits
Salary at the GS-5 level begins in the upper $20,000's.
Salary at the GS-7 level begins in the mid $30,000's.
Salaries listed above do not include compensation for overtime.
Benefits include health and life insurance, savings and retirement plans.

Contact Information
U.S. Customs Service
Office of Human Resources
P.O. Box 14156
Washington, DC 20044
www.customs.gov
www.usajobs.opm.gov/dhscareers/

U.S. Customs and Border Protection
1300 Pennsylvania Avenue
Washington, D.C., 20229
www.cbp.gov

Source: U.S. Department of Homeland Security

UNITED STATES MARSHAL

Description
U.S. Marshals team with federal, state, and local law enforcement agencies to conduct investigations and apprehend fugitives. They also provide protection for federal courts including the security and safety of judges, court officials, jurors, and witnesses. The Witness Security Program is run by the U.S. Marshal Service. Marshals also facilitate the transportation and holding of those awaiting verdict on a federal offense. Transportation of designated individuals may involve moving a prisoner or suspect to and from federal court within state boundaries, state-to-state, or internationally. When needed, Marshals also oversee jail and prison conditions.

Requirements
U.S. Citizen.
Physically fit.
Between the ages twenty-one to thirty-seven.
Applicants must meet one of the following requirements:

Bachelor's degree.
Three years work experience.
Combination of college and work experience.

Training
Fourteen weeks training including eight weeks at the Federal Law
Enforcement Training Center in Glynco, Georgia, and a six-week intensive
U.S. Marshal's Service basic training program.

Salary and Benefits
Salary not including locality or overtime compensation.
GS-5 pay scale upper $20,000's to mid $30,000's.
GS-7 pay scale mid $30,000's to upper $50,000's.
Benefits include health and life insurance plan, sick and vacation pay,
retirement and savings plan.

Contact Information
U.S. Marshals Service
Washington, DC. 20530-1000
www.USmarshals.gov
www.usdoj.gov/marshals/career

Also call district office in your area.

Source: U.S. Department of Labor, Bureau of Labor Statistics,
Occupational Outlook Handbook 2006-2007 Edition
U.S. Marshals Service

UNITED STATES PARK POLICE

Description
U.S. Park Police are responsible for enforcing laws and regulations within
national parks to protect persons and property. Duties include patrol by
foot, vehicle and horse, responding to accidents and emergencies, verifying
park permits and licenses, providing general assistance for visitors, search
and rescue, fire response, and resource protection. Experienced Park Police
officers, can join a Special Forces branch which consists of a SWAT Team
and other criminal investigations units. Park Police are authorized to carry
firearms.

Requirements
U.S. Citizen.
Between the ages of twenty-one and thirty-seven.
Correctable vision to 20/20.
High school diploma or equivalent.
Two years experience dealing with regulation.
Two years of honorable active military duty, two years of college
education, or a combination of both.

Training
Held at the Federal Law Enforcement Training Center in Brunswich,
Georgia, includes firearms training, crowd control, criminal law and
physical conditioning.

Salary and Benefits
Positions after graduation from training typically start in the low $40,000's.
Employees may also receive overtime compensation.
Benefits include health and life insurance, savings and retirement plans.

Contact Information
U.S. Park Police
Personnel Office
1100 Ohio Drive SW
Washington, DC 20242
202-619-7056
www.doi.gov/u.s.park.police

U.S. Office of Personnel Management
1900 E. Street NW
Washington, DC 20415
www.opm.gov

Source: U.S. Park Police

UNITED STATES SECRET SERVICE PHYSICAL SECURITY SPECIALIST

Description

Responsibilities include providing protection for the President and his family, Vice President and family, Former Presidents and family, Potential Presidential and Vice Presidential candidates and their families, visiting foreign government officials and their families, and conducting investigations of counterfeit operations and financial crimes. Expertise is demonstrated by providing physical security through evaluation, design, and installation of countermeasures including technical surveillance, fire and life safety, explosive and chemical/biochemical/radiological countermeasure, and access control systems.

Requirements

U.S. Citizen.
Must be no older than thirty-seven years of age.
Experience in electronics.
Must pass a background investigation including a polygraph test.
Medical and drug screening, physical fitness test.
Frequent travel required
GS-7 level: One year of specialized experience equal to the GS-5 level, one year of graduate school, or excellence in academic scholarship (upper one-third of graduating class, overall GPA above a 3.0, 3.5 GPA or above in area study, or a member of a national scholastic honor society).
GS-9 level: One year of specialized experience equal to the GS-7 level, graduate degree, and two full years of graduate education completed.
GS-11 level: One year of specialized experience equal to the GS-9 level, doctoral degree, or three completed years of graduate education leading to a degree.

Training

Two twelve-week training periods in law enforcement and investigative procedures, held at the Federal Law Enforcement Training Center in Glynco, Georgia and the U.S. Secret Service training center in Washington, DC. Receive training in security assessment, crime prevention, intrusion protection systems, and agency policies and directives.

Salary and Benefits
Salaries range $50,000 to $60,000 plus.
Benefits typically include sick and annual leave, paid holidays, and retirement, health, and life insurance plans.

Contact Information
U.S. Secret Service
Personnel Division
1800 G Street, NW Room 912
Washington, DC 20223
202-406-5800
www.treas.gov/usss
www.secretservice.gov

U.S. Office of Personnel Management
1900 E. Street NW
Washington, DC 20415
www.opm.gov

Source: U.S. Secret Service

UNITED STATES SECRET SERVICE SPECIAL AGENT

Description
Responsibilities include providing protection for the President and his family, Vice President and family, Former Presidents and family, Potential Presidential and Vice Presidential candidates and their families, visiting foreign government officials and their families, and facilitating investigations of counterfeit operations and financial crimes.

Requirements
U.S. Citizen.
Between the ages of twenty-one and thirty-seven.
Bachelor's degree or three years of experience, two of which must be in criminal investigations or a combination of college and work experience.
Vision uncorrected no worse than 20/60 in each eye; correctable to 20/20 in each eye. (Note: The Department of the Treasury has deemed Lasik, ALK, RK and PRK corrective eye surgeries as acceptable eye surgeries for special agent applicants provided specific visual tests are passed one year after

surgery. Applicants who have undergone Lasik surgery may have visual tests three months after the surgery.)

Excellent health and physical condition.

Must pass the Treasury Enforcement Agent or U.S. Marshal's Enforcement exam.

Complete background investigation to include in-depth interviews, drug screening, medical examination, and polygraph examination.

Applicants who are members of the Military Reserve or National Guard will be required to change to either Retired Reserve or Stand-by Reserve status, or shall be discharged as appropriate.

Recruitment Bonus paid to those having foreign language skills.

Training

Two twelve-week training periods in law enforcement and investigative procedures, held at the Federal Law Enforcement Training Center in Glynco, Georgia and the U.S. Secret Service training center in Washington, DC. Agents are trained specifically in criminal, constitutional, and civil law, rules of evidence, courtroom etiquette, report writing, protection, criminal investigation procedures, surveillance techniques, undercover operations, emergency medicine, use of firearms, self-defense and control tactics, physical conditioning, and defensive driving skills.

Salary and Benefits

Salaries begin at the GS-5, GS-7, or GS-9 level depending on qualifications and/or education.

Also receive Law Enforcement Availability Pay (LEAP) that entitles special agent to receive an additional 25 percent of their annual pay. These salary estimates do not include locality pay nor overtime compensation.

Benefits include sick and vacation leave, paid holidays, and retirement, health, and insurance plans.

Contact Information

Contact your local U.S. Secret Service field office, 800-897-8613, or visit the website www.secretservice.gov.

U.S. Secret Service
Personnel Division
1800 G Street, NW Room 912
Washington, DC 20223
202-406-5271

Submit one of the following to the address provided:
1. An Application for Federal Employment SF-171.
2. The Optional Application for Federal Employment OF-612 and a Declaration of Federal Employment OF-306.
3. A resume and a Declaration of Federal Employment OF-306.
Applicants are required to pass the TEA exam, a credit record check, drug screening, polygraph test, background investigation, physical/medical testing, and interviews.

Source: U.S. Secret Service

UNITED STATES SECRET SERVICE UNIFORMED OFFICER

Description
The Uniformed Division officers provide protection for the United States President, Vice-President, President-elect, Vice-President-elect, their immediate families, former Presidents, their spouses and minor children until the age of 16, visiting foreign heads of states/governments, their accompanying spouses, major Presidential and Vice Presidential candidates, their spouses, and others designated by law. In addition, Uniformed Division officers provide protection for the White House Complex, the Vice-President's residence, the Main Treasury Building and Annex, and foreign diplomatic missions and embassies in the Washington, DC area. Uniformed Division officers also travel in support of the Presidential, Vice-Presidential, and foreign heads of state/government missions. Uniformed Division officers are also responsible for the enforcement of mandated protective responsibilities as described under Title 3, United States Code, Section 202.

Requirements
U.S. citizenship.
Must be at least 21 years of age and younger than 37 at time of appointment.
High school diploma or equivalent.
Excellent health and physical condition.

Vision uncorrected 20/60 in each eye; correctable to 20/20 in each eye. (Note: The Department of the Treasury has deemed Lasik, ALK, RK and PRK corrective eye surgeries as acceptable eye surgeries for Uniformed Division officer applicants provided specific visual tests are passed one year after surgery. Applicants who have undergone Lasik surgery may have visual tests three months after the surgery.)

Complete interviews and pass a written test.

Complete background investigation to include driving record check, drug screening, and medical and polygraph examinations.

Positions only available in Washington, D.C.; reasonable moving expenses paid for out-of-area hires.

Employees who are members of the Military Reserve or National Guard will be required to change to either Retired Reserve or Stand-by Reserve status, or shall be discharged as appropriate.

GS-7 level: One year of specialized experience equal to the GS-5 level, one year of graduate school, or excellence in academic scholarship (upper one-third of graduating class, overall GPA above a 3.0, 3.5 GPA or above in area study, or a member of a national scholastic honor society).

GS-9 level: One year of specialized experience equal to the GS-7 level, graduate degree, and two full years of graduate education completed.

GS-11 level: One year of specialized experience equal to the GS-9 level, doctoral degree, or three completed years of graduate education leading to a degree.

Training
Approximately eight weeks of intensive training at the Federal Law Enforcement Training Center (FLETC) in Glynco, Georgia. Upon successful completion of training at FLETC, approximately 11 weeks of specialized instruction at the James J. Rowley Training Center in Laurel, Maryland. Receive training in security assessment, crime prevention, intrusion protection systems, and agency policies and directives.

Salary and Benefits
Starting salary $41,201 per year.
Benefits typically include sick and annual leave, paid holidays, and retirement, health, and life insurance plans.

Contact Information
U.S. Secret Service
Special Agent and Uniformed Support Branch

950 H Street, NW
Washington, DC 20223
202-406-5613
www.treas.gov/usss/opportunities_ud.shtml

U.S. Office of Personnel Management
1900 E. Street NW
Washington, DC 20415
www.opm.gov

Source: U.S. Secret Service

Chapter 3: CAREERS IN THE COURTS

INDUSTRY CONDITIONS AND EMPLOYMENT STATISTICS

Introduction
In terms of careers, the courts provide a range of job opportunities that offer personal and professional satisfaction and reward. The court system is an important forum for the peaceful resolution of conflicts. Whether the issues are pertaining to civil, criminal, or family matters, our courts and the many professionals who work within the courts, are responsible to resolve issues of law in a fair and efficient manner.

Opportunities within the court system are expected to expand, as there is continual court reform and reorganization in efforts to improve the administration of justice. As this change takes place, the staffing needs of the federal, state and local courts will require skilled professionals at all levels. Many of these positions are grouped into job series. In a job series you move from an entry-level position to a higher level or different position within the courts through examinations. Within the court system there are many less known positions such as: Court Administrator, Executive Assistants, Interpreters, Analysts, Clerks, and other courtroom and judge support staff. Before we discuss some of these common careers in detail, let's take a look at the general employment outlook for several high-profile careers – Attorney, Judge, and Paralegal.

Employment Outlook for Attorneys
According to the Bureau of Labor Statistics *Occupational Outlook Handbook* 2006-2007 Edition:

> Employment of lawyers is expected to grow above all occupations through 2014, primarily as a result of growth in the population and in the general level of business activities. Job growth among lawyers also will result from increasing demand for legal services in such areas as health care, intellectual property, venture capital, energy, elder, antitrust, and environmental law. In addition, the wider availability and affordability of legal clinics should result in increased use of legal services by middle-income people. However, growth in demand for lawyers will be limited as businesses, in an effort to reduce costs,

increasingly use large accounting firms and paralegals to perform some of the same functions that lawyers do.

Competition for job openings should continue to be keen because of the large number of students graduating from law school each year. Graduates with superior academic records from well-regarded law schools will have the best job opportunities.

Because of the keen competition for jobs, a law graduate's geographic mobility and work experience assume greater importance. The willingness to relocate may be an advantage in getting a job, but to be licensed in another state, a lawyer may have to take an additional State Bar Examination.

Lawyers held about 735,000 jobs in 2004. Approximately 3 out of 4 lawyers practiced privately, either as partners in law firms or in solo practices. Most salaried lawyers held positions in government or with corporations or nonprofit organizations. The greatest number of lawyers working in government were employed at the local level. In the Federal Government, lawyers work for many different agencies, but are concentrated in the Departments of Justice, Treasury, and Defense. Many salaried lawyers working outside of government are employed as house counsel by public utilities, banks, insurance companies, real estate agencies, manufacturing firms, and other business firms and nonprofit organizations. Some also have part–time independent practices, while others work part-time as lawyers and full-time in another occupation.

Trends in Graduate Employment — 1985-2004

The tables below show employment trends for new law graduates from 2000 to 2004. It is evident that, some decline in the overall employment rate since 2000, the market for new law graduates has been quite strong in recent years. More than half of employed graduates obtain their first job at a law firm — a fact that has not changed in the 31 years that NALP has compiled employment statistics.

Employment Trends
2001-2004

OF THOSE FOR WHOM EMPLOYMENT STATUS WAS KNOWN, % of Jobs in Law

Year	% Employed	% Employed Legal Full-time	% Employed Legal Part-time	% Employed Other Full-time	% Employed Other Part-time	% Not Working	% Pursuing Advanced Degree	% of Jobs in Law Firms
2001	90.0	75.9	6.0	5.5	1.5	7.6	2.4	57.8
2002	89.0	75.3	5.2	5.8	1.6	8.5	2.5	58.1
2003	88.9	73.7	6.5	5.7	1.6	8.4	2.7	57.8
2004	88.9	73.2	7.5	5.3	1.4	8.6	2.5	56.2

Jobs for New Law Graduates – Trends for 1994-2004

According to the ABA, over the past 11 years, the enrollment of both women and minorities in law school has increased fairly steadily, with the enrollment of women rising from 43% to 49%, and minority enrollment increasing from about 15% to about 20%. While the overall graduating classes have been nearly evenly split between men and women, white men have outnumbered white women, but minority women have outnumbered minority men.

NALP's employment data for the classes of 1994-2004 reflect these changing demographics; however, in some job categories, women and minorities continue to be significantly under-represented, while in others, women and minorities are over-represented.

- In firms of 2-10 lawyers, the proportion of jobs obtained by white men has declined (from 55% to 46%), while the proportion of jobs taken by minorities, particularly minority women, has increased. Nonetheless, relative to their numbers among employed graduates, white men continue to obtain a disproportionate share of these jobs, while minorities obtain a smaller share.

- In contrast, the share of jobs in large firms obtained by minority women has increased in most years since 1994; the share obtained by minority men has declined somewhat in recent years. The share of jobs taken by white men has decreased from about 49% in 1994 to 42% in the past two years.

- Prosecutorial positions at all levels of government have consistently been a good source of employment for minorities, particularly minority women, and, to a lesser extent and not as consistently, white women.

- Jobs in the military present a unique demographic profile. In 1994, two-thirds of these jobs were obtained by white men. After dropping to about 57% in 1997 and 1998, this figure has returned to over 60% in all of the past six years except 2002. Thus, white men continue to be over-represented among graduates obtaining these jobs. (It is worth noting that in 1991 and 1992, not shown because of space limitations, the representation of white men was even higher C over 70%.) This is true for minority men as well, although fluctuations are evident. Conversely, despite a modest gain overall, women, particularly white women, remain under-represented among those obtaining jobs in the military.

- The representation of white women among federal judicial clerks generally has been slightly more than proportional, whereas the opposite is true of minority women in most years. Minority men have generally been under-represented.

- The percentage of state judicial clerkships obtained by women has consistently exceeded their representation among employed graduates as a whole, whereas white men have been under-represented. Minority men are also under-represented; the presence of minority women, however, mirrors that among employed graduates as a whole.

Employment Outlook for Judges
According to the *Occupational Outlook Handbook* 2006-2007
Edition:

> Overall employment of judges, magistrates, and other
> judicial workers is projected to grow about <u>as fast as
> average</u> for all occupations through 2014. Budgetary
> pressures at all levels of government will down the hiring
> of judges, despite rising caseloads, particularly in federal
> courts. Most job openings will arise as judges retire.
> However, additional openings will occur when new
> judgeships are authorized by law or when judges are
> elevated to higher judicial offices.
>
> Public concerns about crime and safety, as well as a
> public willingness to go to court to settle disputes, should
> spur demand for judges. Both the quantity and
> complexity of judges' work have increased because of
> developments in information technology, medical
> science, electronic commerce, and globalization. The
> prestige associated with serving on the bench will ensure
> continued competition for judge and magistrate positions
> However, a growing number of judges and candidates for
> judgeships are choosing to forgo the bench and work in
> the private sector, where pay is significantly higher.
>
> Employment of arbitrators, mediators, and conciliators is
> expected to grow about as fast as the average for all
> occupations through 2014. Many individuals and
> businesses try to avoid litigation, which can involve
> lengthy delays, high costs, unwanted publicity, and ill
> will. Arbitration and other alternatives to litigation
> usually are faster, less expensive, and more conclusive,
> spurring demand for the services of arbitrators, mediators,
> and conciliators. Administrative law judges also are
> expected to experience average growth in employment.

Salaries among judges vary significantly from state to state and
among the various levels of the judicial system. According to the
Bureau of Labor Statistics, the highest paid judges earn more than

$141,750 dollars. The lowest paid judges could earn less than $30,000 dollars. Nationally, the median annual wage for all judges was $93,070 dollars.

Employment Outlook for Paralegals
Paralegals and legal assistants, held about 224,000 jobs in 2004. Private law firms employed 7 out of 10 paralegals and legal assistants; most of the remainder worked for corporate legal departments and various levels of government. Within the Federal Government, the U.S. Department of Justice is the largest employer, followed by the Social Security Administration and the U.S. Department of the Treasury. A small number of paralegals own their own businesses and work as freelance legal assistants, contracting their services to attorneys or corporate legal departments.

According to the Occupational *Outlook Handbook* 2006-2007 Edition:

> Employment for paralegals and legal assistants is projected to grow much faster than average for all occupations through 2014. Employers are trying to reduce costs and increase the availability and efficiency of legal services by hiring paralegals to perform tasks formerly carried out by lawyers. Besides new jobs created by employment growth, additional job openings will arise as people leave the occupation. Despite projections of rapid employment growth, competition for jobs should continue as many people seek to go into this profession; however, experienced, formally trained paralegals should have the best employment opportunities.

> Private law firms will continue to be the largest employers of paralegals, but a growing array of other organizations, such as corporate legal departments, insurance companies, real estate and title insurance firms, and banks will also continue to hire paralegals. Demand for paralegals is expected to grow as an increasing population requires additional legal services, especially in areas such as intellectual property, healthcare, international, elder, sexual harassment, and environmental law. The growth of

prepaid legal plans also should contribute to the demand for legal services.

Job opportunities for paralegals will expand in the public sector as well. Community legal-service programs, which provide assistance to the poor, aged, minorities, and middle-income families, will employ additional paralegals to minimize expenses and serve the most people. Federal, state, and local government agencies, consumer organizations, and the courts also should continue to hire paralegals in increasing numbers.

THE JOBS

This section provides basic information about five common careers in the courts. Each job entry includes a brief general description, basic employment requirements, typical training requirements, salary/benefits information, and contact information. To learn more about these and other related positions, we encourage you to contact the agencies and organizations listed.

<u>ATTORNEY</u>

Description
Lawyers, also called *attorneys*, act both as advocates and advisors in our society. As advocates, they represent one of the parties in criminal and civil trials by presenting evidence and arguing in court to support their client. As advisors, lawyers counsel their clients concerning their legal rights and obligations, and suggest particular courses of action in business and personal matters.

Attorneys practice in civil or criminal law in the role of prosecuting or defense counsel. They are trained to interpret and apply the law based on the purposes of laws and prior judicial decisions. Their role is to present the facts of the case as they know it to the court. They spend much of their time researching and examining the evidence and facts of their current case in comparison with cases that been decided before that have changed or created laws in order to gauge how to present their case. Some specialty areas of law are environmental, international, bankruptcy and probate, and intellectual property law. Most lawyers are in private practice, representing civil and criminal cases but may also represent state and federal agencies or nonprofit agencies. Lawyers who work for state attorneys general, prosecutors, public defenders, and courts, play a key role in the criminal justice system. At the federal level, attorneys investigate cases for the U.S. Department of Justice and other agencies. Government lawyers also help develop programs, draft and interpret laws and legislation, establish enforcement procedures, and argue civil and criminal cases on behalf of the government.

Requirements
Bachelor's degree.
Juris Doctorate degree from an ABA accredited school.
Pass their state written BAR exam.
Some states require passing written ethics examination.
Must have good communication skills, verbal and written, and acute analytical and researching abilities.

Training
Law students often acquire practical experience by participation in graduate school sponsored legal clinic activities; in the school's moot court competitions, in which students conduct appellate arguments; in practice trials under the supervision of experienced lawyers and judges; and through research and writing on legal issues for the school's law journal. They typically learn their practice by example within their first few years on the job.

Salary and Benefits
In 2004, the median annual earnings of all lawyers were $94,930. The middle half of the occupation earned between $64,620 and $143,620. Median annual earnings in the industries employing the largest numbers of lawyers in May 2004 were as follows: Management of companies and enterprises - $126,250; federal government - $108,090; legal services - $99,580; local government - $73,410; and state government - $70,280.

Contact Information
For federal employment, contact the U.S. Office of Personnel Management.

U.S. Office of Personnel Management
1900 E. Street NW
Washington, DC 20415
www.usajobs.opm.gov

For nonfederal employment, contact the organization of interest directly for job availability.

American Bar Association
321 North Clark Street
Chicago, IL 60610
www.abanet.org

Law School Admission Council
P.O. Box 40
Newton, PA 18940
www.lsac.org

National Association for Law Placement
1025 Connecticut Avenue
NW, Suite 1110
Washington, DC 20036

Source: U.S. Department of Labor, Bureau of Labor Statistics, *Occupational Outlook Handbook* 2006-2007 Edition

COURT ADMINISTRATOR

Description
Responsible for court administration and management, with regard to casework, court staffing, and fiscal matters. Employment can be found at local, state, and federal levels. Court Administrator usually assists the Chief Judge; provides administrative oversight with respect to the court calendar and supervises the preparation of reports, statistical studies, court security, and other activities to ensure the proper assignment and disposition of court cases.

Requirements
Bachelor's degree, often requires graduate education.
U.S. Citizen.

Training
Training is offered at many higher education institutions, the Institute for Court Management of the National Center for State Courts, and the Court Executive Development Program.

Salary and Benefits
Salaries typically start at approximately $54,000.

Contact Information
National Center for State Courts
300 Newport Avenue
Williamsburg, VA 23185
800-616-6164

U.S. Office of Personnel Management
1900 E. Street NW
Washington, DC 20415
www.opm.gov
www.usajobs.opm.gov

Source: U.S. Office of Personnel Management

COURT REPORTER

Description
Court Reporters work in courtrooms and outside the courtroom for both legal and private organizations, documenting proceedings as official transcripts using a stenotype machine, which is commonly fed into computer-aided transcription. Employment may be found through a court or organization, though reporters often work as independent contractors. Court Reporters typically take verbatim reports of speeches, conversations, legal proceedings, meetings, and other events when written accounts of spoken words are necessary for correspondence records, or legal proof. Job prospects are expected to be excellent as job openings continue to outnumber job seekers.

Requirements
Qualifying examination for state licensing, which includes testing on skills and knowledge (terminology and reference), dictation, and transcription.
The National Court Reporters Association (NCRA) requires 225 words per minute.
Many states require state certification, which is a certified court reporter degree.
Most reporters own their own equipment.
Some states require court reporters to be notary publics.

Training
Two- and four-year programs at postsecondary technical and vocational schools.
Must have excellent listening skills, as well as good English grammar and punctuation skills. Must also be aware of business practices and current events.

Salary and Benefits
According to the *Occupational Outlook Handbook* 2006-2007 Edition, court reporters had median annual earnings of $42,920. The middle 50 percent earned between $30,680 and $60,760. The lowest paid 10 percent earned less than $23,690, and the highest paid 10 percent earned over $80,300.

Contact Information
Contact the local, state, or federal court in your area.

U.S. Office of Personnel Management
1900 E. Street NW
Washington, DC 20415
www.opm.org
www.usajobs.org Job listing

National Court Reporters Association
8224 Old Courthouse Road
Vienna, VA 22182
www.ncraonline.org

American Association of Electronic Reporters Association.
23812 Rock Circle
Bothell, WA 98021

United States Court Reporters Association
P.O. Box 465
Chicago, IL 6069-0465
800-628-2730
www.uscra.org

Source: U.S. Department of Labor, Bureau of Labor Statistics,
Occupational Outlook Handbook 2006-2007 Edition

JUDGE/MAGISTRATE

Description
Judges are responsible for applying the law and ensuring that hearings and trials are conducted in fairness to all parties involved. Pretrial hearings are conducted to hear allegations, evidence and facts of the case, and a judgment is made if the case merits a trial. If there is a jury trial, the judge is responsible for instructing the jury as to their role and responsibilities. A judge decides a sentence in a criminal case and a penalty in a civil case. Judges also manage the court administration and staff. Federal judges are nominated by the President and confirmed by the Senate. Half of all state judges are appointed; positions can also be attained by election. State and local judges serve terms but some may be lifetime appointments.

Requirements
Bachelor's degree and a Juris Doctorate degree required.
Work experience as an attorney.
Federal Administrative judges must be lawyers and pass a competitive exam.

Training
Judicial training is provided by the Federal Judicial Center, the ABA, National Judicial College, and National Center for State Courts. Most states require continuous education.

Salary and Benefits

Judges, magistrate judges, and magistrates had median annual earnings of $93,070 in May 2004. The middle 50 percent earned between $54,140 and $124,400. The top percent earned more than $141,750, while the bottom 10 percent earned less than $29,920. Median annual earnings in the industries employing the largest numbers of judges, magistrate judges, and magistrates in May 2004 were $111,810 in state government and $65,800 in local government. Administrative law judges, adjudicators, and hearing officers earned a median of $68,930, and arbitrators, mediators, and conciliators earned a median of $54,760.

In the federal court system, the Chief Justice of the U.S. Supreme Court earned $280,100 in 2005, and the Associate Justices earned $199,200. Federal court of appeals judges earned $171,800 a year, while district judges had salaries of $162,100, as did judges in the Court of Federal Claims and the Court of International Trade. Federal judges with limited jurisdiction, such as magistrates and bankruptcy court judges, had salaries of $149,132.

According to a 2004 survey by the National Center of State Courts, salaries of chief justices of state high courts averaged $130,461 and ranged from $95,000 to $191,483. Annual salaries of associate justices of the state highest courts, averaged $126,159 and ranged from $95,000 to $175,575. Salaries of state intermediate appellate court judges averaged $122,682 and ranged from $94,212 to $164,604. Salaries of state judges of general jurisdiction trial courts averaged $113,504 and ranged from $88,164 to $158,100.

Contact Information

The National Judicial College
Judicial College Building/358
University of Nevada, Reno
Reno, NV 89557
800-255-8343
www.judges.org

National Center for State Courts
300 Newport Avenue
Williamsburg, VA 23185
800-616-6164

Source: U.S. Department of Labor, Bureau of Labor Statistics,
Occupational Outlook Handbook 2006-2007 Edition

PARALEGAL

Description
Paralegals assist lawyers in doing much of the background work for cases.
Responsibilities include researching laws, prior cases, investigating facts
and evidence, writing legal documents and briefs, coordinating
communications, and keeping records of all documents.

Requirements
Depending on the firm or employer, a college degree or a paralegal
certificate from a two or four-year program may be required. If the area of
law is specialized, the applicant may be required to have either collegiate or
work related experience, such as tax law or real estate law. To become a
Certified Legal Assistant, applicants must pass a two-day examination
given by the National Association of Legal Assistants. To become a
Registered Paralegal, applicants must pass the Paralegal Advanced
Competency Exam issued by the National Federation of Paralegal
Association (this requires a bachelor's degree plus two years experience as a
paralegal). Both certifications provide better opportunity for employment
and salary.

Training
Employers often provide internal training including law and legal research
training techniques, and information on specialty areas of the law.

Salary and Benefits
In 2004, full-time, wage and salary paralegals and legal assistants had
median annual earnings of $39,130. The middle 50 percent earned between
$31,040 and $49,950. The top 10 percent earned more than $61,390, while
the bottom 10 percent earned less than $25,360.

Contact Information
Contact the local, state, or federal court in your area, U.S. Office of
Personnel Management, or law firm directly.

U.S. Office of Personnel Management
1900 E. Street NW
Washington, DC 20415
www.opm.org
www.usajobs.opm.gov

National Federation of Paralegal Associations
P.O. Box 33108
Kansas City, MO 64114
816-941-4000
www.paralegals.org

Information on paralegal training programs, including the pamphlet "How
to Choose a Paralegal Education Program," may be obtained from:
American Association for Paralegal Education
Legal Assistant Management Association
2965 Flowers Road South, Suite 105
Atlanta, GA 30341
770-457-7746
www.aafpe.org

Source: U.S. Department of Labor, Bureau of Labor Statistics,
Occupational Outlook Handbook 2006-2007 Edition

PRETRIAL SERVICES OFFICER

Description
United States Pretrial Service Officers are responsible for gathering information
and preparing reports for judges who must decide whether arrested persons should
be released before trial in the federal court system. The pretrial services officer
has duties and responsibilities similar to those of a probation officer on the federal
level. Officers will supervise defendants who are released and are responsible for
notifying the courts of violations of pretrial release. They assist persons under
supervision with social service referrals, monitor pretrial release reports for the
U.S. Attorney, and maintain effective interagency liaisons when required.

Assistance is provided in pretrial diversion cases, which involve court supervision agreements as an alternative to prosecution. As law enforcement personnel, U.S. Pretrial Service Officers are authorized to carry firearms.

Requirements
U.S. Citizens
At least 21 years old and no older than 37 years old.
Bachelor's degree in criminal justice, psychology, sociology and one year of specialized experience relating the probation, pretrial services, parole, corrections, criminal investigation, or work in substance abuse treatment. (Experience as a police patrol officer or security officer is not acceptable). Qualifying specialized experience may be substituted by excellent academic achievement and completion of a Master's degree.

Training
U.S. Pretrial Services Officers attend an orientation training program at their placement site followed by seminars at the Federal Judicial Center in Washington, D.C. which provide an overview of federal court operations, sentencing guidelines, and reporting procedures.

Salary and Benefits
Appointment to grade CL-25 at the Bachelor's level (CL-25 is similar to GS-7 level)
Beginning salary upper $20,000's to mid $30,000's.

Contact Information
Pretrial Services
Administrative Office of the U.S. Courts
1 Columbus Circle, NE
Washington, D.C. 20544
www.uscourts.gov

Source: Federal Pretrial Services office

Chapter 4: CAREERS IN CORRECTIONS

INDUSTRY CONDITIONS AND EMPLOYMENT STATISTICS

Introduction

Despite a nationwide drop in the overall crime rate through the 1990's, the number of persons in the correctional system continues to grow. This increase can be observed at the federal, state, and local level, as illustrated by the following data from the Bureau of Justice Statistics:

- At the end of 2000, the U.S. adult correctional population – including persons in jail, in prison, on parole, and on probation – totaled 6.5 million. This represents a 3.1 percent of all U.S. adult residents or 1 in every 32 adults.
- There were an estimated 486 prison inmates per 100,000 U.S. residents in 2004 -- up from 411 at year end 1995.
- At mid-year 2004, 713,990 inmates were held in the Nation's local jails, up from 691,301 at mid-year 2003.
- The number of women under the jurisdiction of state or federal prison authorities increased 4.0% from year end 2003, reaching 104,848 and the number of men rose 1.8%, totaling 1,391,781.
- Between 1970 and 2000, the U.S. juvenile population declined from 32 million to 27 million, then rebounded to nearly 32 million again.
- Over half of the increase in state prison population since 1995 is due to an increase in the prisoners convicted of violent offenses.
- At year end 2004, over 4.9 million adult men and women were under federal, state, or local probation or parole jurisdiction; approximately 4,151,100 on probation and 765,400 on parole.

Given these statistics, it is not surprising that of the three major criminal justice functions – law enforcement, corrections, and the courts – direct expenditures for corrections saw the greatest increase nationally from 1995-2001. States spend more on criminal justice than municipalities, counties, or the federal government. For better or worse, there is a significant job growth for corrections professional of all types – from correctional officers to parole and probation officers to social workers. In fact, the Bureau of Labor Statistics ranks corrections officer in the top 25 of all occupations for projected numerical job growth between 1996 and 2006. The Bureau predicts that over 100,000 new corrections officer positions will be created during that ten-year span.

According to the Bureau's *Occupational Outlook Handbook* 2006-2007 Edition:

Job opportunities for correctional officers are expected to be excellent. The need to replace correctional officers who transfer to other occupations, retire, or leave the labor force, coupled with rising employment demand, will generate thousands of job openings each year. In the past, some local and state corrections agencies have experienced difficulty in attracting and keeping qualified applicants, largely due to relatively low salaries and the concentration of jobs in rural locations. This situation is expected to continue.

Employment of correctional officers is expected to grow more slowly than the average for all occupations through 2014. The adoption of mandatory sentencing guidelines calling for longer sentences and reduced parole for inmates will continue to spur demand for correctional officers. However, mandatory sentencing guidelines are being reconsidered in many states because of a combination of budgetary constraints, court decisions, and doubts of their effectiveness. Expansion and new construction of corrections facilities are expected to create new jobs for correctional officers, although state and local government budgetary constraints could affect the rate at which new facilities are built and staffed. As a result employment of correctional officers will probably grow at a slower rate than in the past. Some employment opportunities also will arise in the private sector as public authorities contract with private companies to provide and staff corrections facilities.

Layoffs of correctional officers are rare because of increasing offender populations. While officers are allowed to join bargaining units, they are not allowed to strike.

Correctional officers held about 457,000 jobs in 2000. Almost 6 of every 10 jobs were in state correctional institutions such as prisons, prison camps, and youth correctional facilities. About 15,000 jobs for correctional officers were in federal correctional institutions, and about 19,000 jobs were in privately owned and managed prisons.

The states with the largest percentages of their adult populations under correctional supervision were Georgia (6.8 percent), Texas (5.0 percent) and Idaho (4.9 percent). The states with the smallest percentages of their populations under supervision were West Virginia, New Hampshire and North Dakota (0.9 percent). Almost a third of all people under correctional supervision were in a prison or a jail. More than half of the correctional populations in Mississippi (58 percent), Virginia (56 percent) and Vermont (11 percent) had the lowest percentage of incarceration.

In most professions, salaries in the corrections field vary significantly from state to state. According to 2001 data from the Bureau of Labor Statistics, the highest paid full-time corrections officers and jailers are employed in Alaska, New York, New Jersey, California, Massachusetts, and Oregon. In all of these states, the median annual salary was between $37,700 and $54,800. The lowest paid corrections officers and jailers work in Mississippi, Tennessee, Louisiana, Kentucky, West Virginia, and Arkansas. In these states, median annual wage was less than $25,000.

Expenditure and Employment Statistics
States spend more on criminal justice than municipalities, countries, or the federal government between 1982-1999. Direct expenditure for each of the major criminal justice functions (police, corrections, judicial) has been increasing from 1982-1999.

- In fiscal year 2001, federal, state, and local governments spent over $167 billion for police protection, corrections, and judicial and legal activities, a 7% increase over 2000. For every resident, the three levels of government together spent $600.

- State and local governments combined spent 85 percent of all direct justice dollars in 2001; the federal Government spent the remaining 15 percent.

- The federal government alone spent more than $25 billion on criminal and civil justice in 2001, state governments spent nearly $59 billion, and local governments spent over $83 billion.

Parole and Probation

Parole and probation programs have come under heavy fire recently from politicians and public interest groups who claim that these programs put the public at risk and do not effectively rehabilitate convicted criminals. Despite this growing movement (which includes the adoption of truth-in-sentencing laws by many states), the number of convicted criminals on probation and parole in the U.S. continues to grow.

According to the Bureau of Justice Statistics, nearly 4.6 million adult men and women were on probation or parole at the end of 2000, an increase of almost 70,700 during the years. The 1.6% decrease in this population from 1999 to 2000 was less than the average annual increase of 3.6% since 1990. On December 31, 2000, approximately 3,839,500 adults were under federal, state, or local jurisdiction on probations and about 725,500 were on parole. 2004 saw a 0.5% growth in the probation and parole population which is less than a fifth of the average annual increase of 3.0% since 1995.

Nationwide, women comprised 23% of adult probations in 2000, up from 18% in 1990, and 12% of all parolees, up from 8% in 1990. At the end of 2004, 56% of adults on probation were white, 30% were black, and 12% were Hispanic; 40% of parolees were white, 41% were black, and 18% were Hispanic.

Sixteen states reported less than 1 percent of their adult populations on probation. Three states had increases of at least 10 percent in their probation populations during 2000—Mississippi (up 13 percent), South Dakota (up 11 percent) and Oklahoma (up 10 percent). Nine states and the District of Columbia reported a decline in their probation populations, led by South Carolina (down 12 percent), Missouri (down 5 percent) and Kansas (down 5 percent).

Parole population gains of 10 percent or more were reported in 14 states and the District of Columbia. Connecticut and Arkansas led with a 22 percent increase in their parole populations in 2000, followed by Vermont and Oklahoma (both up 20 percent). Nineteen states reported a decline in their parole population during 2000, led by Kansas (down 35 percent) and North Dakota and North Carolina (both down 24 percent).

Given the overall national increase in these two correctional populations, it is not surprising that the Bureau of Labor Statistics predicts "above average" growth in the number of probation and parole officer positions between 1996 and 2006. As the above state statistics imply, however, state-by-state variation can be expected.

THE JOBS

This section provides basic information about six common corrections positions. Each job entry includes a brief general description, basic employment requirements, typical training requirements, salary/benefits information, and contact information. To learn more about these and related positions, we encourage you to contact the agencies and organizations listed.

Please note many social workers operate under different job titles such as Caseworker. Other common job titles in these sub-fields reflect the rehabilitative emphasis of a particular position. Examples include Pre-Release Program Counselor, Juvenile Justice Counselor, Vocational/Employment Counselor, Substance Abuse Specialist, and Recreation Counselor.

CORRECTIONAL OFFICER

Description
Most correctional officers are employed in large regional jails or state and federal prisons. Corrections officers are responsible for monitoring arrestees awaiting trial and those who have been imprisoned. General duties include monitoring activities of prisoners, enforcing rules and maintaining order, and inspecting correctional facilities and prisoners for illegal substances. Most correctional officers are employed in state and federal prisons and are responsible for watching over the 1.4 million offenders who are incarcerated at any given time. Officers are responsible for documenting their findings verbally and in writing. Due to the security needs of prisons e.g., requiring 24-hour surveillance, officers work in shifts, often requiring evening and weekend duty. Officers may be promoted to emergency response task forces, inmate transportation, and security investigations. Employment can be found in police and sheriff departments in county and municipal jails or under federal and state prison agencies. Correctional officers in local jails admit and process about 12 million people a year, with approximately 700,00 offenders in jail at any given time. In 2000, 457,000 correctional officers were employed across the

nation. Correctional officers usually work an 8-hour day, 5 days a week, on rotating shifts. Because prison and jail security must be provided around the clock, Correctional officers work all hours of the day and night, weekends, and holidays. In addition, officers may be required to work paid overtime.

Requirements
Eighteen to twenty-one years of age (varies depending on state).
U.S. Citizen.
Must have a high school diploma or equivalent.
No prior felony convictions.
Must be in good health; eyesight, hearing, and physically fit.
Applicants are screened for drug use, subject to background checks, and required to pass a written examination.
The Federal Bureau of Prisons requires one of the following to obtain a position at the GS-5 pay scale:
1. Bachelor's degree.
2. Three years work experience.
3. Undergraduate experience and work experience that equals that of three years.

Training
Federal requirement of 200 hours of training (120 hours at the Federal Bureau of Prisons Training Center in Glynco, Georgia). State requirements average six weeks of training. Training can include coverage of regulations and operations, custody and security procedures, institutional policies, weaponry, physical training, and emergency response.

Salary and Benefits
Federal entry-level employment begins at $26,747.
Federal and state median salary is $44,700, ranging from $24,000 to $49,000.
Supervisory positions begin at $41,000.
Median salary for first-line supervisors/managers was $44,720 in 2004.
Benefits include medical insurance, vacation and sick pay, and pension plan.
Employees can retire at age 50 after 20 years of service or at any age after 25 years of service.

Contact Information
For information on entrance requirements, training, and career opportunities for correctional officers at the federal level contact:
The Federal Bureau of Prisons, 800-347-7744 or visit www.bop.gov/

To obtain information about a position as a correctional officer with the Federal government visit www.usajobs.opm.gov.

For Federal employment opportunities contact:
Federal Bureau of Prisons, www.bop.gov/
Mid-Atlantic Regional Office   301-317-3211.
North Central Regional Office   888-251-5458
Northeast Regional Office   800-787-2749
South Central Region   214-224-3389
Southeast Region   888-789-1022
Western Region   925-803-4700

For information about correctional jobs in a jail setting contact:
American Jail Association
2053 Day Rd, Suite 100
Hagerstown, MD 21740
301-790-3930
www.corrections.com/aja/

National Institute of Corrections
320 First Street, NW
Washington, DC 20534
800-995-6423
www.nicic.org/inst/
American Correctional Association
4380 Forbes Boulevard
Lanham, MD 20706
301-918-1800
www.corrections.com/aca/

Sources: Federal Bureau of Prisons
Occupational Outlook Handbook 2006-2007 Edition
www.bls.gov/oco/

Also, consider researching:
California Department of Corrections
New York Commission of Corrections
Texas Department of Corrections
Michigan Department of Corrections
Florida Department of Corrections
Illinois Department of Corrections

CORRECTIONAL TREATMENT SPECIALIST*

Description
Correctional treatment specialists, sometimes known as case managers, perform correctional casework in an institutional setting. Correctional treatment specialists work in jails, prisons, and parole or probation agencies. Specialists develop, evaluate, and analyze program needs and other data about the inmates, evaluate progress of individual offenders in the institution, coordinate and integrate inmate-training programs, and evaluate positive and negative aspects in each case. Correctional treatment specialists also provide case reports to the U.S. Parole Commission, work with prisoners, their families, and interested persons in developing parole and release plans, and work with the U.S. probation officers and social agencies in developing and implementing release plans for programs for selected individuals. Employment of correctional treatment specialists is projected to grow as fast as the average for all occupations through 2014. Openings will be created by growth and replacement needs as large numbers of these workers begin to retire.

* This position is listed in conjunction with that of Probation Officer in the *Occupational Outlook Handbook* 2006-2007 Edition.

Requirements
U.S. Citizen.
Must be 21 years of age and no older than 35 years of age (37 years of age for Federal employment).
Bachelor's degree needed with 24 semester hours of social sciences or two years of graduate study in social sciences, or two years of graduate education and casework experience. Graduate education must have been in corrections or a related field, i.e., criminal justice, sociology, psychology, counseling social work.

Training

Newly appointed Correctional Treatment Specialists are provided with an orientation to the mission, policies, procedures, and rules of the agency, as well as an overview of the parole process, parole laws and regulations, professional contacts, and an introduction to Federal Bureau of Prisons and the U.S. Probation operations.

Salary and Benefits

Bachelor's level positions typically start at GS-5 level (salary beginning low $20,000's); for Master's level positions typically start at GS-9 level (salary beginning low-mid $30,000's), and Ph.D. level positions typically start at GS-11 level (salary beginning low-mid $40,000's). As of 2004, the median annual earnings of correctional treatment specialists were $39,600. Higher wages tend to be found in urban areas.

Application Process

Check the Office of Personnel Management website at www.usajobs.opm.gov for employment opportunities.

Contact Information

Federal Bureau of Prisons
320 First Street, NW
Washington, D.C. 20534
www.bop.gov/

United States Parole Commission
Department of Justice
5550 Friendship Blvd., Suite 420
Chevy Chase, MD 20815
301-492-5990
www.usdoj.gov/uspc/

Sources: Federal Bureau of Prisons
Occupational Outlook Handbook 2006-2007 Edition
www.bls.gov/oco/

PAROLE OFFICER

Description
A parole officer is responsible for the legal custody of an offender, after they are released from incarceration, and making sure they abide by the conditions of their release to parole. Parole officers provide counseling and support to help parolees reenter society. Duties include educating the offender on parole guidelines, monitoring parolee behavior through phone calls, visits, electronic reporting, drug screening and keeping written reports of parolee activities for the court and law enforcement agencies. Employment can be found through the federal government under the administrative office of the U.S. Courts, state employment is usually under either a parole board or department of corrections.

Requirements
Bachelor's degree with a major in one of the social sciences and one to three years of experience, or prior experience in parole or probation.
Valid driver's license.
No prior felony convictions.
Written and oral examinations are typically required.
Background investigation.
Drug screening.
Social work and counseling background necessary.

Training
Training conducted under the department of corrections or parole board.
Training in firearms is also required.

Salary and Benefits
Average starting salary is $38,150 - $59,010.
Median annual earnings of all parole officers in 2004 were $38,150.
Median annual earnings for parole officers employed in State government were $36,980; those employed in local government earned $40,820.

Contact Information
American Probation and Parole Association
The Council of State Governments
P.O. Box 11910
Lexington, KY 40578
859-244-8203

www.appa-net.org

U.S. Office of Personnel Management
1900 E. Street NW
Washington, DC 20415
www.usajobs.opm.gov

Sources: U.S. Office of Personnel Management
California Department of Corrections
Michigan Department of Corrections
Florida Department of Corrections
Nevada Parole and Probation.

PROBATION OFFICER*

Description
Probation officers are responsible for counseling and rehabilitating offenders without the use of incarceration. Probation officers supervise offenders on probation or parole through personal contact with the offenders and their families. They also evaluate crimes, make recommendations to the court, and facilitate a probation agreement between the offender and the federal, state, or local court. Responsibilities include monitoring offender behavior, maintaining records of each offender and his or her progress, and reporting to the court of jurisdiction on the offender's status. Employment can be found under the administrative office of U.S. Courts, and state probation or judicial branches. About 84,000 people were employed as probation officers in 2000. Currently, California and Texas have the highest probation and parole populations. Together, these two states account for about one-fourth of the country's correctional supervision population. Employment of probation officers is projected to grow as fast as average through 2014.

* This position is listed in conjunction with that of Correctional Treatment Specialist in the *Occupational Outlook Handbook* 2006-2007 Edition.

Requirements
U.S. Citizen.
Must be 21 years of age and no older than 35 years of age (37 years of age for Federal employment).

Must be familiar with computers used in probation and parole work.
Must have strong writing skills.
Bachelor's degree needed in social work, criminal justice, or related field, and/or experience in probation of intermediate corrections.
Some states require one year of work experience in a related field or one year of graduate study in criminal justice, social work, or psychology.
Valid driver's license.
Drug screening.
Medical and psychological screening.
No prior felony convictions.

Training
Most probation officers are required to complete a training program sponsored by their State government or the Federal government.
Training is typically conducted under the state department of corrections or parole board.
Most positions require six months of training.

Salary and Benefits
Starting salary varies depending on locality but averages between $38,000 to $50,000.
Median annual earnings of probation officers in 2004 were $39,600. In 2004, medial annual earnings for probation officers employed in state government were $36,980; those employed in local government earned $40,820.
Benefits typically include medical and life insurance, holiday and sick pay, deferred compensation plans, and annual leave.

Contact Information
American Probation and Parole Association
The Council of State Governments
P.O. Box 11910
Lexington, KY 40578-1910
859-244-8203
www.appa-net.org

U.S. Office of Personnel Management
1900 E. Street NW
Washington, DC 20415
www.usajobs.opm.gov

Sources: Occupational Outlook Handbook 2006-2007 Edition
U.S. Office of Personnel Management
California Department of Corrections
Michigan Department of Corrections
Florida Department of Corrections
Nevada Parole and Probation.

SOCIAL WORKER

Description

Social workers practice in a variety of settings: hospitals, mental health, community centers, schools, social service agencies, courts, and correction facilities. Social workers help people address and cope with their personal, social and community problems, which can include substance abuse, chronic disease, financial distress, unwanted pregnancy, antisocial behavior, employment stress, and family dysfunction. Social workers are typically specialized in their capacity such as clinical/mental, policy and planning, hospital, juvenile, criminal justice (often pretrial services), and occupational work. Full time social workers usually work a standard 40-hour week; however, some occasionally work evenings and weekends to meet with clients and handle emergencies. Employment in the field of social work is expected to increase faster than the average for all occupations through 2014.

Requirements

Minimum requirement of a bachelor's degree in social work (BSW) from a school accredited by the Council on Social Work Education. A master's degree in social work (MSW) is necessary for positions in health and mental health settings and typically is required for certification for clinical work.

State licensing and certification is typically required. The multiple-choice examinations are given by the American Association of State Social Work Boards. The exams are given by level: Basic, Intermediate, Advanced, and Clinical. As of 2004, the Council on Social Work Education (CSWE) accredited 442 BSW programs and 168 MSW programs. Social Workers held about 562,000 jobs in 2004.

Salary and Benefits
Median annual earnings of child, family, and school social workers were
$34,820 in 2004. Median annual earnings of social workers employed by
state governments were $35, 070 in 2004; those employed by local
governments earned $40,620.

Contact Information
National Association of Social Workers
750 First Street NE, Suite 700
Washington, DC 20002
202-408-8600
www.naswdc.org

American Association of State Social Work Boards
400 South Ridge Parkway, Suite B
Culpeper, Virginia 22701
800-225-6880
www.aswb.org

Council of Social Work Education
1725 Duke Street, Suite 500
Alexandria, VA 22314
www.cswe.org

Sources: Occupational Outlook Handbook 2006-2007 Edition
www.bls.gov/oco/

WARDEN

Description
Responsible for the administrative and organizational control of a
designated prison through the supervision, security and facilitation of
training inmates and planning, directing, and coordinating programs.
Duties also include communications with persons outside the institution,
and enforcing rules and regulations for the safety, health, and protection of
both inmates and the community.

Requirements
BA/BS degree, master's degree preferred.

Must have excellent managerial skills.
Knowledge of all phases of corrections operations.
Pass a background investigation and interview.
Must not be older than thirty-seven years of age.
U.S. Citizen.

Training
Two hundred hours of formal training, eighty hours of Institutional
Familiarization, 120 hours of specialized training at the residential training
center in Glynco, Georgia which includes firearms training, self-defense, a
written test, and a physical abilities test.

Salary and Benefits
Federal salary is at the GS-15 pay schedule $75,000 to $97,000 (this salary
does not include locality pay increases).
Life and health insurance plans, retirement plan, vacation and sick leave.

Contact Information
For federal employment opportunities contact the Federal Bureau of Prisons
at their home page www.bop.gov or by calling your regional office:

1. Mid-Atlantic Regional Office   301-317-3100
2. North Central Regional Office   913-621-3939
3. Northeast Regional Office   215-521-7301
4. South Central Region   214-224-3389
5. Southeast Region   678-686-1200
6. Western Region   925-803-4700

National Institute of Corrections
320 First Street, NW
Washington, DC 20534
800-995-6423
www.nicic.org/inst/

American Correctional Association
4380 Forbes Boulevard
Lanham, MD 20706
301-918-1800
www.corrections.com/aca/

Source: Federal Bureau of Prisons

Chapter 5: RESEARCHING AND APPLYING FOR JOBS

Introduction
There are hundreds (if not thousands) of publications, organizations, and web sites aimed at helping you find and land your dream job. Only a small fraction of these focus on employment in the criminal justice field. However, even the most generalized employment resource--such as *Job Hunting for Dummies* or Monster.com--will offer sound strategic advice that you can apply to your criminal justice job search. A quick, casual look through the Careers section of your local book store will reveal not only the large number of self-help books on this broad topic, but also the significant overlap in the suggestions offered by these publications. If you find one that suits your individual style and needs, we encourage you to use it in conjunction with this text.

This chapter does *not* attempt to cover all aspects of an effective employment search. Instead, it focuses on a few key areas often overlooked, avoided, or misunderstood by job seekers. These include networking, internships, the Internet, and the "dos and don'ts" of resume and cover letter writing. For further reading on these and other related topics, we suggest you consult *Seeking Employment in Criminal Justice and Related Fields, Fourth Edition* by J. Scott Harr and Kären Hess (Wadsworth). Another useful resource is Wadsworth's *Careers in Criminal Justice* interactive CD-ROM, release 3.0.

NETWORKING

Networking is a vital, central component of any effective job search. This practice will keep your job search dynamic and alive, thus avoiding the stop-and-go cycles of answering newspaper ads and browsing job boards. *The American Heritage Dictionary* defines networking as:

> An informal system whereby persons having common interests or concerns assist each other, as in the exchange of information or the development of professional contacts.

In the context of your criminal justice employment search, networking is the practice of using your existing job connections to unearth additional job connections. Successful networking will give you an ever-growing roster of contacts, one of whom will be the person who eventually offers you the position you've been searching for. It can be a tiring and frustrating process, but it's well worth the effort.

There are many reasons why some job seekers resist this practice. First, some of them view networking as dishonorable because it seems to reward the best "schmoozers" rather than the most qualified candidates. This is a narrow, self-defeating view of networking. If this is your perspective, remember that an employer cannot identify you as the most qualified candidate unless you make contact with him or her. *Networking* is the best way to get to that person.

Others shy away from networking because they think they have no connections to start with. Well, if you are reading this book, then you probably have at least three valuable starting points. First, consider your criminal justice instructors. The vast majority of people who teach criminal justice courses have extensive job experience in their chosen field, often with organizations located near their college or university. Don't be shy about asking these instructors for advice and names of people to talk to. They will usually be happy to help.

Another excellent starting point is your school's career center. In fact, your school's criminal justice department may have a career library of its own. In addition to job listings, career centers often collect contact information for alumni who are willing to talk with students about their professions. We highly encourage you to make the most of these connections. The added advantage of these contacts is that they have *volunteered* to speak with students, so you know they'll be receptive to you.

Friends and family represent the third (and most underused) source of professional contacts. For example, if your Uncle Ted has a friend who is a state trooper and that job interests you, you owe it to yourself to make the most of that connection. Don't be embarrassed about it, either. Be assertive and respectful; the results may surprise you. Leave no stone unturned, no opportunity unexplored.

Once you have made a contact or two, the "trick" is to obtain other leads from these individuals. This should be a routing part of all your job-related communication. Even if a contact seems like a dead end, be sure to ask that person if they know anyone else (inside or outside their organization) who might be willing to speak with you. There are many advantages to this approach.

First, you will obtain contact information for people who you might have overlooked or with whom you are not already familiar. You might even discover entire departments or organizations this way. Second, you can use the initial contact's name to capture the attention of your new contact. Whether you initiate communication by phone or letter or e-mail, it's always best to lead with a name that's familiar to the person you're addressing. An opening like "Detective Jones suggested I contact you..." is much more effective than the typical cold call that comes out of nowhere.

Networking can also help you set up *informational interviews*, another valuable investment of your job search time. Unlike interviews for specific advertised positions, informational interviews are less formal meeting during which you can ask questions about a person's job and organization, giving you more information on which to base your career choices. For example, after speaking with a few public defenders, you may find that a private legal practice is more appealing to you. It also gives you a chance to show your enthusiasm and qualifications to a potential employer even when there are no suitable positions currently available. When an appropriate job opens up, an impressive informational interview gives your contact a better sense of your interests and skills, which will help them direct you to other job contacts. Remember, the goal is to obtain at least one additional contact from every person you connect with.

Finally, an often overlooked advantage of networking is that it will help you uncover jobs that have not been advertised yet. It often takes an organization days or weeks to post a new job opening. Advance information through word-of-mouth is invaluable in giving you a head start over the competition. It not only puts you first in line for consideration, it also shows your resourcefulness and go-getter attitude, not to mention your communication skills.

Keep in mind that in order to network effectively you must be organized. A wide range of products can be very helpful--from "day planner" notepads to hand-held electronic organizers or PDAs to computer software. Your networking efforts can (and should) result in an ever-growing web of people, organizations, and events to keep track of. Don't let it overwhelm you. Control it and use it to your advantage.

THE VALUE OF INTERNSHIPS

A more direct approach to networking may include applying and completing an internship during your college experience. An internship provides you with the opportunity to work in a position in your field of interest and gives you an inside perspective of the field. There are many important reasons to complete an internship:

- Hands-on experience in your field of study
- Integrate classroom knowledge into practice
- Learn to develop mentoring and professional relationships
- Interact with people in different positions within your field
- Develop connections for possible future job placement
- To get a start in competitive fields
- Build your resume with work experience
- Identify strengths/weaknesses for future development
- Understanding your role as a member of a team
- Improve your oral and communication skills
- Learn self-reliance and independence
- Develop leadership skills
- Gain self-confidence

Finding an Internship

Finding an internship position in your field of study might be easier than you think. Your college has many resources that you can explore when looking for an internship. Most colleges have an academic advising department and/or a career center, and many colleges have internship offices. All of these offices can be helpful resources for finding internships in careers that pertain to your major fields of study, and often have information from previous students who have completed internships at the specific sites.

Additional resources at your college include faculty and staff. Professors are often approached by internship sites for referrals of qualified students for placements. Many colleges have career fairs where employers recruit for both job opportunities and internships. The alumni office may have contact names of graduates who would consider assisting current students in an internship position. Finally, all college libraries have various resources including reference books and current periodicals that have detailed information on internship positions available in your area of interest.

Outside of the college, you might want to consider some direct exploration including contacting a company directly or researching their website for possible internship opportunities. Lastly, you may want to invest some time in exploring professional associations and organizations related to your field. These organizations often have information and listings of internship positions both within the associations and in the larger work community. For example, the U.S. Office of Personnel Management has a website, www.studentjobs.gov, that specializes in job, internship, and scholarships opportunities for students.

INTERNET RESEARCH

The job-specific contact information in Chapters 2 through 4 of this text includes web site addresses for dozens of organizations. Each site contains valuable information about the sponsoring organization, and many of them offer job listings. However, these are not the only on-line resources that can facilitate your job search. Let's start with the all-in-one career sites. Some of the web sites listed below may already be familiar to you:

America's Job Bank	www.ajb.org
Career Builder	www.careerbuilder.com
Career Journal	www.careerjournal.com
Careers at Yahoo	www.careers.yahoo.com
College Grad Job Hunter	www.collegegrad.com
Department of Defense Jobs	www.dod.jobsearch.org
Employment Guide	www.employmentguide.com
Hot Jobs	www.hotjobs.com
Job Bank USA	www.jobbankusa.com
Job Central National	www.jobcentral.com
Employment Network	
Job Market	www.jobmarket.nytimes.com
Monster.com	www.monster.com
Nation Job	www.nationjob.com
Technology Careers	www.dice.com
True Careers	www.truecareers.com
Washington Jobs	www.work.wa.gov
Work Tree	www.worktree.com

While these and dozens of other comprehensive sites offer an abundance of career resources and job listings, their usefulness to you depends on two things: 1) the geographical scope of your search, and 2) which area of criminal justice you are interested in.

It should come as no surprise that a nationwide job database such as Career Builder probably wouldn't be the most effective tool if you were hoping to find a job in your current place of residence, especially if it is not a large city. When your search is locally focused, it isn't worth spending too much time sorting through thousands of national listings. You can get lucky, of course, but your time would be better spent exploring local resources. If you are hoping--or at least willing--to relocate, then these national databases will probably be more useful. Their usefulness depends on what kind of job you're looking for.

If you're seeking a position in law enforcement or corrections, web sites such as those listed above probably won't yield many appropriate job listings. For example, police departments don't tend to use these kinds of careers services. (The one possible exception to this is Monster.com which seems to offer a relatively larger number of police job listings.) There are, however, many other on-line resources for law enforcement jobs, as you will read below.

If you are seeking a position in the courts, you are more likely to find what you are looking for at one of the above-referenced sites. Advertisements for paralegals and attorney positions are common, especially for those jobs in large private practices located in large metropolitan areas. Again, you will get more out of these listings if you are willing to relocate.

Criminal Justice Employment Web Sites
Scouring the web for criminal justice employment information can be a daunting and frustrating task. To ease this process, we have assembled a list of web site addresses that you might find helpful. Some offer only job listings, while others offer career advice, sample materials (resumes, cover letters, etc.), and/or links to other resources. We encourage you to explore several of these sites.

Law Enforcement

Careers in Government	www.careersingovernment.com
Cop Career	www.copcareer.com
Employment portal	www.911hotjobs.com
Federal Employment	www.usajobs.opm.gov
Federal Government Employment	www.fedworld.gov
Federal Job Search	www.federaljobsearch.com
Guide to Law Enforcement	www.jobs4police.com
Index for Law Enforcement Fire Jobs	www.jobsfed.com/rp/cgi
IRS Careers	www.jobs.irs.gov
Jobs for Women in Law Enforcement	www.womenandpolicing.org/jobs.asp
Law Enforcement Careers	www.policeemployment.com
Law Enforcement Jobs	www.theblueline.com
Law Enforcement Jobs	www.lawenforcementjobs.com/content
Missouri Law Enforcement Online	www.virtuallibrarian.com/moleo/
Nationals Center for Women & Policing	www.womenandpolicing.org/ jobs.asp
NYPD Recruitment	www.nypd2.org/html/recruit/policeofficer
Officer.com	www.officer.com/recruiting
Police Career	www.policecareer.com
Student Jobs in Federal Government	www.studentjobs.gov
USA Jobs	www.usajobs.opm.gov
Web's Best Job Search Resources	www.job-hunt.org/law.shtml
911 Hot Jobs	www.lawenforcementjob.com

The Courts

Attorney Jobs	www.attorneyjobs.com
Court Job Description Database	www.ncsconline.org/D_KIS/ jobdeda/main.htm
Law Employment Center	www.lawjobs.com
Nation Job Network	www.nationjob.com/legal/
Nationwide Drug Court Job Bank	www.nadcp.org/coordinators
New York State Unified Court System	www.courts.state.ny.us/careers/US
The Legal Employment Search Site	www.legalemploy.com/
US Courts Employment Database	www.uscourts.gov/employment/

Corrections

American Correctional Association Job Bank	www.aca.org/jobbank/
Community Corrections Job Opportunities	www.doc.wa.gov/HRRecruiting/ community_corrections.htm
Corrections & Criminal Justice	community_corrections.htm

95

RESUMES AND COVER LETTERS

No matter how you find that perfect job listing, you will need to send your potential employer a resume and cover letter. Probably the most important thing about a resume is that even a great one won't win you that job, but a lousy one will take you out of the running in a heartbeat (even if you're well qualified). The same is true for cover letters.

Again, there are hundreds of publications, services, and web sites out there that can help you put together a great resume and cover letter. This section does not attempt to cover everything there is to know about preparing these materials. For further information, we encourage you to consult your local library or career center. We will, however, review a few of the key "dos and don'ts" you should keep in mind when writing your resume and cover letter.

Resumes

Perhaps the most important trap to avoid is lying on your resume. While you are encouraged to present your experiences and achievements in ways that sound impressive, do not include anything that simply is not true. Not only would it be unethical, but getting caught in a lie is the easiest way to eliminate yourself from consideration. As much as any other profession, the criminal justice field is founded on honesty and integrity so you must be truthful at all times.

If you are unsure about whether something you've written crosses over the exaggeration line, imagine yourself being asked about it in an interview. Would you be able to discuss it confidently and without hesitation? If not, then you should definitely tone it down a bit.

Two common ways to make your resume more dynamic are to use action words as much as possible while avoiding the passive voice. For example, instead of saying that you were "given the job of store manager," state that you "managed all store functions." While these phrases mean basically the same thing, the latter version suggests greater responsibility and energy on your part. You may find the following list helpful as you search for action words:

achieved	conducted	hired	provided
administered	consulted	indentified	researched

analyzed	controlled	inspected	scheduled
applied	coordinated	investigated	selected
approved	decided	led	served
arranged	designed	managed	set up
assessed	developed	monitored	solved
assisted	established	operated	supervised
built	evaluated	organized	taught
chaired	examined	planned	trained
completed	guided	produced	wrote

Another important trap to avoid is over-stuffing your resume. While it may seem intuitive that a longer resume is more impressive, keep in mind that employers can receive hundreds of resumes for a single job so they often won't even take the time to read one that's too long. Try to limit your resume to one page. Your resume should only require a quick scan to give the reader a good idea of your background. You can always fill in the details during your interview. Hit the highlights, eliminate the fluff. Remember, "less is more."

Finally, you should ask a number of people to review your resume. This can include professors, friends, professional contacts, career counselors, etc. Every bit of feedback helps. It will take you a few drafts to work out the kinks and getting a fresh perspective will help you tremendously. Your resume should be easy for everyone to understand--even people with little or no experience in the criminal justice field.

Two sample resumes are provided at the end of this chapter for reference (see pages 99-100). For more resume construction advice, we encourage you to read Chapter 9 of Harr and Hess' *Careers in Criminal Justice and Related Fields: From Internship to Promotion, Fifth Edition* (Wadsworth).

Cover Letters
You should never submit a resume by itself. All resumes and other submissions must be accompanied by a cover letter, even if it is a very brief one. Here are a few things to keep in mind:

- Whenever possible, address your cover letter to a specific individual, not an entire organization or division. Packages and letters addressed to "Personnel Department" or "To Whom It May Concern" may never find their way into the right hands.

- If you got the recipient's name through networking, be sure to open your cover letter with an acknowledgement of the source, e.g., "Judge John Larimer suggested that you would be a good person to contact...". This association will help you get noticed by the reader. If it also helpful to send a copy (cc:) of the letter to your networking source. This will reinforce your connection with that person while showing them that you have taken action and followed their advice.

- Like a resume, a cover letter should be brief and to the point. Limit all letters to a single page--preferably no more than three-quarters of the sheet. Again, employers often have to sift through hundreds of cover letters and resumes so they will tend to avoid longer documents.

- Find out as much as you can about the job before writing your cover letter. Not only will this show the reader that you've done your homework, it will also help you tailor the letter to bring out those elements of your background that make you a standout candidate.

- Don't restate your entire resume in your cover letter. Let the resume do its job. You should, however, point the reader to one or two key resume highlights that relate directly to the job(s) you're applying for.

- When writing a follow-up letter after an interview, don't just thank the person for their time. Try to recall something from the conversation that was especially significant to you. This will help the recipient remember your conversation while showing him or her that you are attentive and focused.

- A cover letter/resume is an employer's first opportunity to evaluate your writing ability. Most jobs in the criminal justice field require solid communication skills. A cover letter that includes unclear thoughts, spelling errors, incorrect grammar, and/or typos will reflect negatively on your ability to communicate in writing. If you are applying for a writing-intensive job, even a single mistake may eliminate you from consideration. Proofread your letters carefully. Ideally, you should ask at least one other person to review each letter before you send it out.

A sample cover letter and a follow-up letter are provided at the end of this chapter for reference (see pages 101-102).

98

Sample Resume #1: Historical/Chronological

ISABELLE L. GARCIA
621 Anthony Drive
New York, NY 10112
Phone: 716-224-7364
E-mail: igarcia@zipnet.com

OBJECTIVE: To obtain a challenging career opportunity in the field of international criminal justice.

EDUCATION:

2002-2006   JOHN JAY COLLEGE OF CRINIMAL JUSTICE
New York, NY
Bachelor of Arts
- Major - International Criminal Justice

2002   FONTBONNE HIGH SCHOOL
Brooklyn, NY
High School Diploma
- Honors - Regents Diploma

WORK EXPERIENCE:

2004 to present   SECURITY GUARD, Xerox Corporation
New York, NY:
Maintain security for a busy downtown office complex. Responsibilities include front desk check-in, metal detector supervision, video system monitoring, and corridor patrol. Work day and night shifts. Carry sidearm while on duty.

2002-2004   ANIMAL HANDLER, Frenchtown Animal Hospital
Frenchtown, NY:
Provided animal management assistance in a large veterinary hospital. Duties included feeding and exercising pets, maintaining enclosures, controlling dangerous animals, and monitoring hospital grounds.

REFERENCES: Available upon request.

Sample Resume #2: Functional

ISABELLE L. GARCIA
621 Anthony Drive
New York, NY 14435
Phone: 716-224-7364
E-mail: igarcia@zipnet.com

OBJECTIVE

To obtain a challenging career opportunity in the field of criminal justice.

PROFESSIONAL EXPERIENCE

2003 to present   **Monroe County International Airport**, Rochester, NY:
Security Officer
Hired as a uniformed security officer. Duties include metal detector/x-ray machine monitoring, video surveillance, corridor patrol, and passenger assistance. Train new security personnel in use of detection devices and communication systems. Serve as liaison between airlines, vendors, and local law enforcement. Work with airport managers to assure compliance with federal security regulations. Lead special security details for visiting dignitaries and other high-risk passengers.

2000-2003   **Penfield Furniture Works,** Penfield, NY:
Assistant Manager
Hired as a truck driver/delivery person. Promoted to stock manager, then assistant manager. Duties included ordering materials, scheduling shipments, tracking distributor accounts, addressing customer complaints, and training new employees.

EDUCATION

2004-2006   **State University of New York,** Genesco, NY:
Bachelor of Science – *Police Studies*

2005   **Kings County Public Defender's Office,** Brooklyn, NY:
Internship

2002-2004   **Monroe Community College,** Rochester, NY:
Associate of Art – *Law Enforcement Certification*

References available upon request.

Sample Cover Letter

ISABELLE L. GARCIA
621 Anthony Drive
New York, NY 10112
Phone: 716-224-7364
E-mail: igarcia@zipnet.com

October 11, 2006

Captain Armando Franco
Rochester Police Department
117 Main Street
Rochester, NY 14239

Dear Captain Franco,

The purpose of this letter is to express my interest in the police officer position advertised in last Sunday's Democrat and Chronicle. Since earning my bachelor's degree in criminal justice from John Jay College of Criminal Justice this past June, I have been serving as an intern with the Wayne County Office of New York State Highway Patrol. I am confident that this training, combined with my three years experience as a Kodak Park security guard, makes me an ideal candidate for your department.

I have enclosed a copy of my resume for your review. If you require additional information, please contact me at the above address.

Thank you for your time and consideration. I look forward to your reply.

Sincerely,

Isabelle L. Garcia

Encl.

Sample Follow-Up Letter

ISABELLE L. GARCIA
621 Anthony Drive
New York, NY 10112
Phone: 716-224-7364
E-mail: igarcia@zipnet.com

June 21, 2006

Ms. Juliette Patrix
Human Resources Department
DeLucia Protective Services, Inc.
7680 University Avenue
Bronxville, NY 10708

Dear Ms. Patrix:

Thank you for taking the time to meet with me today. I enjoyed having the opportunity to discuss the various security officer positions currently available. You were very helpful and provided me with valuable information about DeLucia Protective Services.

I was especially interested to learn about the technology training opportunities your company offers new security personnel. I believe that my combination of computer skills and personal security experience make me an ideal candidate for several of the positions we discussed.

Again, thank you for your consideration and I look forward to hearing from you soon. Please let me know if you need any additional information.

Sincerely,

Isabelle L. Garcia